DIOCESE OF DULUTH
2830 EAST FOURTH STREET
DULUTH, MINNESOTA 55812

MARY from Nazareth

RETURN TO: EDUCATION OFFICE
DIOCESE OF DULUTH
2830 EAST 4TH STREET
DULUTH, MN 55812
218.724.9111

MARY
from Nazareth

by
Bruna Battistella

Translated by
Deana Basile

BOOKS & MEDIA

BOSTON

Library of Congress Cataloging–in–Publication Data

Battistella, Bruna.
   [Maria, la conchiglia di Dio. English]
  Mary from Nazareth / Bruna Battistella: translated by Deana Basile.
     p.   cm.
  ISBN 0-8198-4772-0
  1. Mary, Blessed Virgin, Saint—Biography—Juvenile literature. 2. Christian saints—Palestine—Biography—Juvenile literature. 3. Christian saints—Israel—Biography—Juvenile literature. [1. Mary, Blessed Virgin, Saint. 2. Saints. I. Title.]
BT607.B34   1996   96–2694
232.91—dc20   CIP
   AC

Illustrations: Carla Cortesi

Original title: *Maria, la conchiglia di Dio*

Copyright © 1991, Figlie di San Paolo, via Albani 21, 20149 Milan, Italy

English edition copyright © 1996, Daughters of St. Paul

Printed and published in the U.S.A. by Pauline Books & Media, 50 St. Paul's Avenue, Boston, MA 02130.

Pauline Books & Media is the publishing house of the Daughters of St. Paul, an international congregation of women religious serving the Church with the communications media.

1 2 3 4   99 98 97 96

A Note to Parents and Teachers:

In order to present the life of Mary in a way that is both appealing and understandable to young readers, some fictional characters and dialogue have been added to the actual facts provided in the Gospels.

Keep this in mind as you plan

Have you ever been near the ocean during a storm?

I have. At first I was really afraid, but then my fear changed into joy. This is how it happened.

One night there was a lot of noise and confusion. Lightning flashed and thunder roared. The waves were pounding just a few feet from our house. It seemed like they would flood the beach and destroy all the houses. It seemed like all the people living near the beach would be drowned.

But the flood never came and the bad storm died down by the next morning. The sun came out, but it didn't look bright and cheerful like it usually does.

At eleven o'clock I went down to the beach. The sun was still dim. The sky above the water was dark. I walked along the beach. I kept my head down. The cold wind was blowing.

And then I saw...a black ball in the sand. I was curious. I went over to check it out. Slowly I dug the ball out of the sand. It turned out to be an almost perfectly round shell. Its two halves were sealed tight. It was a beautiful shell.

The fierceness of the storm had pulled that shell out of the depths of the sea. The storm had given it to me as a gift. I was even more excited when I pried the shell open and found a tiny pearl inside! Discovering that shell and pearl made me really happy.

This morning I was thinking about you. I picked up my pen and decided to write to you about Mary, the mother of Jesus. I remembered the joy I felt when I discovered my shell. I thought of how my shell is a symbol of Mary, our mother. Let's think about her.

Before I found it on the beach, my shell had been formed under the ocean. It had been shaped, sanded and smoothed until it became the cradle of a precious pearl.

Something like this happened with Mary.

When God created us, he thought of me and you. He thought of Mary in a very special way. He wanted to make her the cradle for his best gift to us. Of course, you know who that is—Jesus!

God always thought about Mary. He wanted to make her beautiful, good and lovable. He wanted to make her full of wisdom and mercy. She would be strong but gentle, full of love for God and for all people. God created Mary just as he wanted her.

One day God placed Mary on the small "beach" of the earth, in a land called Palestine. Because of Mary, the time of fear on earth would end, and the days of love and peace would begin.

We're lucky because we've found this "shell" of God. In this book, we want to learn about Mary. We want to learn about how beautiful she is and about how she became the mother of the most precious "pearl"—Jesus.

I read the Gospel so that I could tell you about Mary. It is called the Gospel but you know that there are really four Gospels. They were written by different men. All four tell the story of Jesus and his mother Mary.

Jesus and Mary lived on earth at a certain time and in a certain place. We learn about the history and customs of their people from the Old Testament. The Old Testament (or Hebrew Scriptures) is the first part of the Bible. The Bible is the most famous book in the world.

The Old Testament is important because it tells the history of the people of Israel. It tells us something about the future, too—about Jesus.

So, to write this story about Mary, I used the Gospels and the Old Testament.

I really hope you enjoy this story. I hope it helps you learn more about Mary, the mother of Jesus.

Table of Contents

Always in God's Thoughts 10
The People of the Promise 13
Isaiah Speaks of Mary 16
Mary's Parents 19
Mary, God's Loved One 25
Mary from Nazareth 28
Mary and the Angel 33
Mary Visits Elizabeth 37
Mary, Joseph's Bride 39
Mary, Jesus' Mother 43
Mary and the Shepherds 47
Jesus, the God Who Saves 51
The Three Wise Men Arrive 55
We Must Save the Baby! 61
Mary in Egypt 66
Mary in Jerusalem 72
Son, Why Have You Done This? 79
Three Hearts in One 85
Mary and the First Miracle 92
The Beginning of a Mission 97
Who Is My Mother? 100
One Saturday at the Synagogue 102
With Jesus as Passover Approaches 104
At the Last Supper 106
With Her Dying Son 109
One Mother for Everyone 112
The Joy of Seeing Jesus Again 116
Mother of the Newborn Church 121
Mary in Heaven 125

Always in God's Thoughts

When God decided to create the universe, he thought about it. Like the best architect, God designed his plan. People were to live in the universe he was going to create. They needed light, heat, water and plants.

God included the stars, the planets, and the oceans in his plan. He designed them to be just the right weight and size. He also planned the orbits of the planets so that the planets wouldn't bump into one another. That would have been the end of the world!

God carried out his plan. Everything came to be in the right place at the right time, just like the pieces of a giant puzzle.

God arranged the stars in systems and constellations. He placed the planets in orbit around their stars. He gathered the waters in oceans and rivers and lakes.

God made the earth a planet of the sun. It would become the home of human beings.

Earth was beautiful. There were mountains and valleys, large plains and lakes. There were long rivers and small streams, and a great number of plants and animals.

When everything was ready, God created the first man, Adam. He formed him from the earth and gave him a soul. From Adam, God formed Eve, the first woman. God made both Adam and Eve in his own "image and likeness."

When Adam saw Eve, he was full of joy. She smiled at him, spoke to him, and walked with him. Adam was very happy. He exclaimed: "This woman has the same flesh and blood as I do."

And he called her Eve.

God said to Adam, "You can eat the fruit of all the trees of the garden. But you must not eat the fruit from the tree of the knowledge of good and evil. If you eat from it, you will die."

Adam and Eve took care of the animals and the plants in the garden. It was fun for them to work together! They were very happy, and thanked God for all that he had given them.

They enjoyed God's visits every day. But one day Eve received a mysterious message. A voice coming from a snake said to her: "You can become like God."

Adam and Eve wanted to be like God and to have the knowledge of good and evil. It was their moment of testing. Adam and Eve could have told God they loved him. They could have told him that he was their God. They could have obeyed the law that God had given them: "Do not eat from the tree of the knowledge of good and evil."

But they didn't.

I think you must have already heard this story about the original sin. ("Original" means "first.") This sin didn't only change the lives of Adam and Eve. It changed the lives of all the people who came after them. It changed your life and my life.

The Bible tells us this story. It tells us that Eve believed the false promise of the snake. She ate the fruit of the forbidden tree, and gave it to Adam who also ate it. Both of them disobeyed God.

Suddenly Adam and Eve were afraid of God. They felt that their friendship with God was broken. When they heard God coming to visit them, they ran off to hide.

God came. He knew that the man and the woman had hidden from him. He knew that they had disobeyed him and that they didn't love him.

God called to Adam: "Where are you?"

From his hiding place, Adam answered, "I am hiding because I am naked."

God said to Adam, "You are hiding because you are naked? Who told you that you were naked? Have you eaten from the tree I told you not to eat from?"

God knew everything. Adam was acting like a child who was caught eating candy before mealtime. He pointed at Eve. "The woman whom you put beside me gave me the fruit of the tree and I ate it." Eve said that she had been tricked by the serpent. According to the Bible story, God condemned the snake. But it was not really a snake. It was the devil, the enemy of God.

As punishment, God said that Eve would feel pain when she gave birth to her children. God said that everyone would have to work hard in order to live. All men and women would have to suffer and die.

At the same time, God made a very special promise to Adam and Eve. Because of his love for them, the Lord had a surprise for the man and the woman. "I will send a Woman who will not listen to the serpent-devil. She will have a son. He will crush the head of the serpent-devil."

God gave Adam and Eve a ray of hope. But they didn't know that the Woman would be Mary.

The People of the Promise

After many years had gone by, God called a rich shepherd named Abraham. He was a descendant of Shem, the son of Noah. Abraham was born in Chaldea. Later on he moved to the city of Haran in upper Mesopotamia.

God said to Abraham, "Leave your country, your relatives and your father's home, and go to a land that I will show you. From you, I will make a great people. I will bless you and you will be a blessing to others. Through you, I will bless all the families of the earth."

Abraham and Sarah didn't have any children, and they were both very old. Abraham still believed, however, that God could make him the head of a great people. Together with Sarah, their servants and their livestock, he left Mesopotamia. Abraham let God guide him to the land of Canaan.

One very starry night, God invited Abraham to come out of his tent. God said to him, "I made you leave Ur so that you would become the head of the land of Canaan. Look at the sky. Can you count all of those stars?... Just like them, your descendants will be so numerous that no one will be able to count them all."

The Lord made a pact of friendship with Abraham. He promised to protect him. God asked Abraham to worship him and be faithful only to him. Abraham swore that he would worship only God.

God kept his promise. He blessed Sarah, as old as she was, and she had a baby boy.

Abraham was happy. He believed that God was the one true God. His faith in the Lord grew. When the child was born, Abraham lifted him to the sky and shouted with joy, "His name is Isaac!" Isaac smiled and so did God. God promised Isaac, too, that he would be the head of a great people.

Isaac grew up and married Rebecca. They had two sons who were twins, Esau and Jacob. These brothers quarreled continually about which one of them would receive the blessing of their father. Whoever got that blessing would also receive the blessing of God.

Jacob was very smart. His mother Rebecca helped him obtain the great blessing of his father.

Isaac said to Jacob:
"God will give you the dew from the sky,
and fertile lands
and a large amount of wheat and wine.
Nations will serve you
and the people will bow down before you—
so will your brother."

Esau grew jealous and angry. So Isaac and Rebecca advised Jacob to go to Haran and stay with his uncle Laban.

Jacob went, and he learned a lot from his life there. Jacob became a shrewd businessman. While he was taking care of his uncle's property, Jacob was also thinking of himself. He married Laban's two daughters, Leah and Rachel. (At that time a man could have more than one wife.) Jacob had a daughter and many sons.

Jacob was happy with his family. He was also happy because he had many cattle. But Jacob wanted to go back to his home. He was afraid, though, that Laban would not let him leave because of Leah and Rachel. So Jacob took his whole family and secretly ran away to Canaan.

Jacob and his children lived in Canaan for many years until a great shortage of food made them go to Egypt. There they found Joseph, Jacob's second youngest son. Joseph had become an important official in Egypt. The pharaoh gave Joseph a very good piece of land for his father and brothers. They grew rich and the whole family became larger and larger.

The children of Jacob became the heads of twelve tribes. These tribes formed the people of Israel. The name Israel had been given to Jacob by God himself.

Jacob's descendants remained in Egypt for four hundred years. At first they were honored by the Egyptians because of the good relations the Egyptians had with Joseph. But, Jacob's descendants were soon made slaves and forced to build cities for the pharaoh. The pharaoh was afraid of the Israelites because there were so many of them. In fact, he had his soldiers kill all of their baby boys.

The Israelites remembered the promise God had made to Abraham. They prayed and cried aloud to their God. They begged him to send someone to free them.

God answered their prayers. He sent Moses to guide them back to the land of Canaan, the promised land.

Under the leadership of Moses, the Israelites crossed the desert of the Sinai peninsula. On Mount Sinai Moses had a wonderful vision of God. God sent the people his ten rules or "commandments," which were his law. The people swore to be the Lord's people and always obey him.

God let the Israelites wander through the desert for forty years. They came to know God better and to feel the love and care that God had for them. When they were thirsty, God made water run from a rock. When they were hungry, he gave them manna and quail to eat. God protected them from poisonous snakes and from the enemies who came to stop their march toward Canaan. God was really their leader.

And yet, the Israelites complained against God. They sinned against his laws. Once the Israelites even made an idol, a golden calf. They worshipped the calf instead of God. God patiently corrected them and forgave them. He stayed with them to fight for them. With God's help the Israelites were able to enter the land of Canaan and conquer it.

Under the leadership of the kings, the priests, and the prophets, Israel became a united people. They had their own laws and customs. Without knowing it, Israel was living out its history of salvation. It was preparing to receive the true Redeemer.

Isaiah Speaks of Mary

Isaiah was the greatest prophet of ancient times. During a difficult time for Israel, he told the king that God would come to help. Isaiah gave the king a sign:

"The virgin will conceive and bear a son, whom she will call Emmanuel. Before the child can learn to judge between good and evil, your enemies will flee. And there will be a time of great well-being for all."

The people listened and thought about it. They didn't really know if the promised baby was the son of the king or another child who

would bring a time of peace to the country. But they remembered the promise about a Woman whose son would conquer the serpent-devil.

There were times when special women, full of faith and courage, performed great deeds. Were any of them the Woman God had promised to send?

We Christians believe that these strong women were like pictures of Mary, who fights against evil and wins.

One of these women was Jael. Her story is told in chapter four of the book of Judges.

The people were still fighting to own Canaan. The Israelites had defeated the king of Hazor, but Sisera, the commander, had managed to escape. While he was looking for a hideout, he met Jael. She allowed him to hide in her tent. She fed him and hid him under a blanket so that no one would find him. But when Sisera fell asleep, Jael gathered up her courage and killed him. Once again the people of Israel were safe from their enemies.

Another brave Jewish woman was Judith (see chapter 13 of the book of Judith). She risked her life to go into the enemy camp outside the city of Bethulia. One night she was invited to supper in the tent of the captain, Holofernes. After he had fallen asleep, she cut off his head.

Judith returned to Bethulia. The Hebrews placed Holofernes' head on the wall of the city. When the enemy soldiers saw it, they became very frightened. They ran away from the city and were killed by the Israelites.

Other Jewish women also remind us of Mary. Mary asks the Lord to have mercy on us.

One of these women was Abigail.

Saul was the first king of Israel. He was chasing David and his soldiers in order to kill them, because he was jealous of David. David and his men had run away and were wandering through the mountains and fields. One day they were very hungry and had no more food. David had always saved the cattle of Nabal (a nearby rancher) from raids, so he sent ten men to ask Nabal for food. But Nabal looked down on David and wouldn't give him the food.

Then David lost his patience. He armed himself, and he and his soldiers started toward the field where Nabal was shearing his sheep. David would have killed Nabal if he hadn't met Abigail,

Nabal's wise wife. Abigail knew what had happened. She took food and wine and put it on some donkeys. Then she went to meet David to calm him down. As soon as Abigail saw David, she got down on her knees in front of him. She begged him not to do any harm. "Someday you will be king of Israel," Abigail said.

David's heart was touched by Abigail's words. He accepted the food that she had brought to him, then he sent her home.

"Return home in peace," David told her. "I listened to your voice and it calmed my spirit."

Abigail was a good peacemaker, and she probably saved her family.

Esther is another woman who was strong and had faith in God.

Esther was a Jewish refugee in Susa. She became the wife of Xerxes, the king of Persia, who chose her to be queen (see chapter five of the book of Esther). One day she went to see the king. She knew that it could cost her her life, because she had not been invited into the king's presence. Esther convinced the king to keep her people from being killed.

Esther risked her own life to save the lives of her people.

God had not forgotten Mary at all. In fact, the actions of Jael and Judith, of Abigail and Esther, tell us something about what Mary's mission would be: to help God's people.

The people sang to Judith:
"You are the glory of Jerusalem.
You are the joy of Israel.
You are the honor of our people."

These words of praise are taken from the Bible. The Church sings them to Mary, the mother of Jesus. She was always present in God's love.

Mary's Parents

The land of Israel had often been invaded by other peoples: Syrians, Babylonians, Egyptians, Greeks and Romans.

Sixty-three years before Jesus was born, the Romans conquered Israel. Six years after Jesus was born, the Romans made Israel a Roman province. There was finally peace throughout the Roman Empire.

God said that this was the right time for the Woman to be born.

God prepared a father and a mother for the Woman. Her parents' names were Joachim and Ann. They were already growing older. They had never had any children. They wanted a child very much, and believed in God's help.

One day, Ann ran up to Joachim. Her face was glowing with joy. She no longer seemed the same. Even the wrinkles around her eyes and forehead had disappeared.

Ann held Joachim close and whispered to him, "We are going to have a baby. Yes, I'm sure of it. God is wonderful; he is giving us a child!"

Joachim was very happy too. Finally God was answering his prayers. Together Ann and Joachim thanked God. If the baby were a boy then he would be able to bear their family name in the assembly of Israel. That would be really wonderful! But Joachim and Ann would accept God's gift of a little girl with the same love and joy. In fact, a girl would be able to help them and comfort them in their old age.

Several months later, the first cries of the long-awaited baby were heard. It was a baby girl.

The friends who had come to help Ann washed the newborn baby. They rubbed her down with salt. This was the custom at that time. They said to Ann: "She's a true Israelite: she has strength in her little arms and legs. God has blessed you. This baby girl is certainly loved by God."

Ann answered: "Yes, God loves her very much." And she cried tears of joy.

Ann and Joachim, like all mothers and fathers, didn't know what their little girl would be like. But they were happy. And since they were sure that God loved their child in a very special way, they wanted to remind her of that for her whole life. So they called her Mary. This name means "God's beloved one."

Every time little Mary cried, Joachim would become worried and would ask, "What can it be?"

"Don't worry Joachim," Ann would answer. "It is feeding time. Mary must be hungry."

Ann would nurse and take care of the baby. She would also play with her with little bells and a cymbal. And Mary would open up her big eyes with delight. Mary was wrapped in swaddling clothes so that she looked like a tiny Egyptian mummy. Every so often Ann would remove these clothes that looked like bandages. She would rub Mary with olive oil and sprinkle her with powder. Mary liked this. She would let out little cries of joy. She seemed to be thanking Ann for taking care of her.

Mary continued to grow. She filled the household and the lives of Ann and Joachim with happiness. Soon, they were also teaching her. They wanted to teach Mary to love God as they did.

Mary was eager to learn and willingly obeyed her parents' wishes.

Mary would go up with her parents to the Temple of the Lord. She liked to pray as her mother did. She stayed right by her side in the women's aisle. Mary loved these visits...the Temple was so beautiful and there was so much hustle and bustle around her.

At that time (five to ten years before Jesus was born) going to the Temple meant meeting many other Jewish people. They came faithfully to offer to God the scent of incense, which was their morning sacrifice. The Temple would be full of workers. The Lord was there to receive his children. The people came to tell God they loved him and to ask his help.

King Herod, who had been placed in power by the Romans, was ruling Palestine. The Jews did not like him because he was cruel and because he was a foreigner. He wanted to gain their respect, so he had the Temple of the Lord

rebuilt. Herod's Temple may have been even more beautiful than Solomon's. It was certainly larger. There was a huge walkway with wide portals on the sides. Even though the beautiful Temple is gone, that walkway is still there today.

Mary was a sensitive and intelligent girl. She enjoyed the liveliness of the courtyards in the Temple. She thought about the history of God's people, and of the Lord's love for them.

Mary knew about this history. Joachim and Ann taught her about it every Saturday. Saturday was the day of the Lord for the Jewish people. On Saturdays, Mary, Ann and Joachim would gather together in the house. Joachim would peacefully sit in a well-lit corner. Ann would not weave or think about the meals that day. She would prepare everything the night before. On Saturday Ann would sit next to her husband. Then Mary would sit on a low stool which her father put out for her and the lesson would begin.

"Father, we're listening."

"So where did we leave off last Saturday?"

Mary would look at Ann as if to say, "Is it my turn?" Yes, it was always her turn because in this school she was the only student. Joachim was the teacher and Ann was the substitute teacher.

But whenever they read the prophecies or the Lord's words there were three students present. That's because when it came to the Word of the Lord, even Joachim and Ann felt like school children.

Ann would motion to Mary who would then say: "Father, you explained…you prayed…you told us about…." She would then explain whatever he had said last. Mary had a very good memory.

Joachim would smile at her. Then he would open a rolled-up parchment and pray to the Lord, using the same words David or one of the prophets had used. Ann and Mary, filled with love for God, would also repeat these words.

Mary always wanted to understand what she was saying. She wanted especially to understand the words she had learned by heart.

"Father," she would ask, "why do we say: 'Let the heavens open up, and let the clouds rain down the Just One. Let the earth open up and salvation come forth'?"

Her father would answer, "We ask the Lord to send us the promised Savior. He will free us from those who try to harm us. But first of all he will come to renew our hearts, so that we will obey him and be pleasing to him."

Mary also wanted to please the Lord. She wanted all of her people to please the Lord.

"The Lord has placed us under the rule of unbelievers," her father would continue. "We haven't obeyed his law and we haven't loved him with all our hearts. Yet the Lord loves us and is faithful to his promises. He will send the Savior to us."

Ann would go on, "The Savior will come from the descendants of King David. He will have a mother who is different from any other mother. His mother will be as pure as a little girl."

Ann's words recalled the prophecy of Isaiah: "The Virgin will give birth to a baby boy. He will be our God among us."

Mary didn't understand why, but it seemed to her that the Lord wanted those words to stay in her heart. When Ann brought her to the Temple, she repeated to the Lord, "Let the heavens open up, and let the clouds rain down the Just One. Let the earth open up and let the Savior come forth. May the Virgin have a son, our God among us."

The memory of the promised Woman and of her son remained in the minds of the Israelites. It was like a red thread which runs through the pattern of a rug.

No one knew what you and I know. No one knew that the red thread which was woven into the history of Israel was Mary—that little girl who used to walk through the streets of Jerusalem with her parents.

No one knew that the sparkling seashell, the cradle of the most beautiful pearl, was that little girl, Mary. She had been chosen by God to be given to all people. She was the young brown-haired girl who used to race up the hill of Sion to be the first to reach God's house.

Don't you think that God would have wanted to give some clue, at least a small one, that Mary was the Woman for whom all of Israel was waiting?...

I think so.

But right now I have one question. I'll whisper it to you. What if there had been a sign? And what if all of us—the people of that time as well as the people of today—didn't even recognize it?

Well, maybe there was a sign, shining like the sun, and no one stopped to notice it. They didn't see it even in the smallest thing, like Mary's innocent eyes, eyes which were different from every other girl's eyes. Before she was born, the Lord himself had made them pure. He wanted to tell everyone that only light lived and would live in that little girl. She was the Immaculate One!

Mary, God's Loved One

Mary went up to the Temple with her heart full of joy. She prayed to the Lord and listened to the story of all the wonderful things he had done for the people of Israel.

Joachim used to tell her about how God's people escaped from Egypt. God had made it possible in a way that only he could have chosen. He had lifted the wind from the east to dry the sea up just enough so that the people could walk across to reach the other side safely. When Mary heard this story, she was filled with gratitude and love for God.

Mary wanted to show her love to God. But she was still so little. Deep inside her heart the Holy Spirit told her that God loves little ones in a very special way. Even though they're not big and can't do big things, their love is enough for him. This message prepared Mary to be what God wanted her to be.

To her parents, Mary seemed so different from the other little girls. They thought that it was because of the great love they had for her. Meanwhile, they prayed for guidance about her future. Little by little they realized that God wanted Mary for himself. Ann and Joachim offered her to God as the most beautiful jewel of their house.

One day Ann and Joachim dressed Mary in a white robe. They placed a veil on her head, with a little crown of white flowers. Then they went to the Temple. Ann was carrying a bright colored candle made of beeswax.

"Let me carry it, Mother!" Mary said, "I want my life to be given only to God, just as the light of this candle will be for him."

Ann and Joachim smiled.

At the entrance of the Temple, a priest came to welcome the little girl. He went to one of the candleholders and lit Mary's candle. Then he placed it in Mary's hands, and walked slowly toward the altar. The little girl followed him. Her face and eyes reflected the light of the candle. She went to the altar and faced the priest who blessed her and prayed:

May the Lord receive you into his love, little Mary.
May he be your protector and your glory.
Through him may your life be exalted
and may your mouth sing him praises.
May he keep his eyes always upon you
and may he give you his grace and glory.
Mary smiled and said:
I want to exalt the Lord, my God
and sing him a new song.
He has remembered his love and the promises which he made to Israel, his people.
For this reason everyone on earth
will see the promised Savior.

The priest bowed and took the candle that Mary offered to him. He put it on the altar, so that it would burn in honor of the Lord. It would burn in memory of the offering Mary had made.

Ann and Joachim cried when Mary returned to them. They led her back home to continue her lessons.

Joachim gave even more attention to teaching his daughter about God. But he still didn't know about the mission God had chosen for her.

Ann taught her to love the poor, to help the suffering, and to respect everyone.

Since Mary was growing up to be a responsible young girl, Ann gave her some small chores to do around the house. She asked her to help with the cooking. She sent her to bring her father's messages to friends or relatives. Ann taught Mary how to embroider. Mary was very good at it. Soon Ann taught her how to spin and weave wool.

Ann was overjoyed. When Mary finished her embroidering, she would speak to her mother about the God of Israel. Ann believed that Mary had seen him or heard his words. God's words filled Mary's soul. In those moments, Ann saw Mary as a "teacher." It didn't matter to her that her student had become her teacher. She understood that the Word of God was Mary's joy.

Joachim liked to hear Mary sing the psalms of the Lord. Mary had learned them from the Levites who sang in the Temple. He was also proud of her when she danced to the sound of the tambourines, in honor of the Lord.

Her friends would often come to ask if Mary could play with them. She took part in the games and made them more fun.

When Mary was around, everything was peaceful and happy. When people saw her love for God and others, they wanted to be kind and full of joy.

In this way, Mary grew in love for the Lord while she lived like every other Jewish girl.

But the day came when Joachim and Ann died. They never had the chance to see the long-awaited Savior. However, they had seen, touched and loved the one who would be his mother. God had made this clear to them. And they rejoiced in this blessing.

Mary from Nazareth

Before I continue with Mary's story, I'd like to take you on a pilgrimage with me to northern Palestine.

We are leaving Jerusalem, which is in the south, in Judea. The Jews love this holy city. They repeat the same words which their exiled brothers used to repeat in Babylon:

If I forget you, Jerusalem, may my right hand be still.
Let my tongue remain silent if I forget
that you are all my joy.

As we pass through Samaria, we see a beautiful mountain, Gerizim. Here the Samaritans worship God. In Shechem we see a famous well, the one which supplied fresh water to Jacob and his children. Far off, toward the sea, is the plain of Sharon and farther north, near the center, the fertile plain of Esdraelon. Toward the east we see the bright blue background of the Gennesaret Sea, which is shaped like a harp. We enter Galilee and discover Mount Tabor. On the other side of Mount Tabor is Nazareth.

Let's stop on this hill to visit this little town which Luke, the Gospel writer, calls a city.

Some boys come up to us, leading their goats along. Who knows where they are going? We follow them and end up at the town's fountain. The goats run to their drinking place, surrounding the sheep who have already arrived there.

A scuffle breaks out among the small shepherds, but the girls who are getting water calm them down.

It's morning and the girls of Nazareth are arriving one at a time, carrying their water jars on their shoulders. We watch them while they approach. They seem to be dancing, with their veils and robes flowing.

The small alleys of the town are bordered with little white houses. Each house has a terrace. Here and there, next to the doors, there are trees: fig trees, sycamores, pomegranate trees, or grapevines.

It is very peaceful here. Wherever we look we see people hard at work. In fact, a blacksmith is busy at work in the open space in front of his house. He's hammering a horseshoe on a donkey. A carpenter is making a simple plow. He's singing as he works.

Every so often, we see along the road an inner courtyard where a woman is grinding grain. Another woman is baking small loaves of barley bread in a clay oven. Under a fig tree a mother is nursing her baby. Next to her an elderly woman is weaving cloth on a loom.

Life in Nazareth is simple because the people are poor. They live on whatever God's land offers, and exchange some of the products that the land produces: oil, olives, grapes and figs.

Even though it is a poor town, Nazareth has its synagogue. The people gather there on Saturdays, the day of the Lord, to honor him and pray to him, to listen to his Word. The rabbi proclaims

God's Word in the Hebrew language and then repeats it in Aramaic. He does this because by this time the Hebrew language has been forgotten by many of the people.

Today, right outside of the synagogue there is a group of children between the ages of six and twelve. They are waiting for the rabbi, who teaches them about the one God. He also teaches them reading and writing. The children are lively and happy, and are playing with each other. A little boy is singing a rhyme. That's how he remembers the teacher's lesson.

While we are approaching, a young girl comes out of one of the small houses. Someone calls to her, "Shalom, Mary!"

"Shalom, Naomi. How's everything with your family?"

"Fine, but you know, Mary, my grandmother is getting old and every day she has a new illness."

"I'll come to see her today. Is that okay?"

"Oh, yes. You know how she loves it when you come to visit."

You know who this is, don't you? The young girl we are meeting in Nazareth is the same Mary who was orphaned in Jerusalem.

Mary was living with her relatives in Nazareth. The Gospels tell us that Mary had many cousins there.

Mary had accepted these changes. She knew that Nazareth was a hidden place which no one was ever interested in. But she was certain that God hadn't forgotten her. She knew that even in Nazareth every orphan had a father in God. And so she had come to Nazareth with faith.

She had left the memories of her childhood in Jerusalem: the house where she was born, next to the sheep pool, the friends she had grown up with, the wonderful festivals she had attended every year with her parents. Now she carried these memories in her heart, together with the happiness she felt at belonging to the Lord.

Her house, like most the houses in Nazareth, was made up of walls which extended from the sides of a cave and formed a room. There Mary lived the normal life of her people. She took care of her household chores and visited her relatives. She went down to the fountain to fetch the water that she needed; and she stayed and talked with other young people there. These friends would often seek her company and work close to her. But most of all they loved to hear about the holy city, Jerusalem, and about the Temple of the God of Israel.

Mary joyfully lived the simple life of Nazareth. She enjoyed seeing the town come alive at the sound of the trumpet which announced the holidays. She loved the prayer groups in the synagogue and the festivals: Passover in the springtime, Pentecost in the beginning of summer, the festival of the booths in the fall, the celebration of lights in December....

Every festival celebrated and honored the love God had shown for Israel. Every Hebrew celebrated this, and so did Mary.

Some festivals lasted for days. The people had to wait until the day of rest to make agreements, buy land, and even make marriage proposals.

It was during one of these celebrations that a young man named Joseph decided to ask Mary to become his wife. Many young men in Nazareth would have gladly taken his place!

In those days, young men and women who were thinking about getting married could not make their own choices. Their relatives decided everything for them.

Mary and Joseph knew one another, of course. Only two or three hundred people lived in Nazareth, so everyone knew each other. Joseph knew how wise, kind and modest Mary was. So he was very happy when the two families agreed about the marriage.

Mary was the one who was shocked. She had wanted to give her heart completely to God. But she believed it was God's will that she marry Joseph, and she became his promised bride.

Joseph was a descendant of David, to whom God had promised an eternal kingdom. But Joseph had inherited only the family name. In order to live, he worked as a carpenter, a trade which he knew well and was very good at. He was modest, reserved and respectful of God's Law. Joseph was really a good man.

Like any good Jew, Joseph wanted to have a baby, a son, who

would be able to defend his people. He wanted his son to be a true worshiper of God, like his ancestor David.

Mary, whom God had placed beside him, would have a son. But Joseph would not be the father.

Without knowing it, Joseph had entered into the mystery of God.

Mary and the Angel

If we had lived near Mary, we would have found her busy at her household duties, as she had been before becoming Joseph's fiancée. Joseph would come to visit her whenever he was able. Mary welcomed him with joy. Together they decided how they would fix up the house where Joseph was living. He would bring Mary to this house as soon as it was ready.

Mary's cousins often came to keep her company and to help her sew her wedding dress. But let's not imagine that it was like the gowns which brides wear today! At that time the brides' dresses were very simple. They were made up of a slip, a veil and a new robe.

The cousins congratulated Mary for being engaged to such a serious young man who came from the family of David. But Joseph certainly didn't dream of becoming a king. At that time there was an Idumean king who ruled but had to obey Imperial Rome. The possibility of becoming king, though, interested the cousins. Even young girls of that time dreamed of handsome princes....

"What do you think, Mary, will God keep his promise to return the throne of Israel to a

descendant of David?" they asked.

"God keeps his promises, our whole history tells us that. But we don't know when the Lord will put his plan into action," Mary answered.

These were serious discussions but they seemed far-fetched. None of the Jewish people's efforts to drive out the conquerors had succeeded. The foreigners had ruled over Israel for many years and had torn the country apart.

But instead...there was an angel of the Lord sent to bring a message of joy to Mary, for Israel and for the people of every nation forever.

Having entered Mary's house, the angel Gabriel said, "I bring you greetings, you who are full of grace. The Lord is with you."

When she heard these words, Mary became scared and asked herself what this could mean.

The angel said to her, "Don't worry, Mary, because God loves you. You will conceive and bear a son and you will call him Jesus. He will be very important and will be called the son of the Almighty. The Lord God will give him the throne of his ancestor, David. He will reign forever over the house of Jacob and his kingdom will never end."

Then Mary said to the angel: "How is it possible? I am not married."

The angel answered: "The Holy Spirit will come upon you. The power of the Almighty will be with you. The one who will be born will be holy, and he'll be called the Son of God. You see, even Elizabeth, your older relative, whom everyone thought could not have children, will bear a child in three months. Nothing is impossible for God."

Then Mary said, "Here I am, the Lord's servant. Let what you have said be done."

And the angel left her.

It's great to read this passage of the Gospel where Luke tells us about the most important event on earth. The Holy Spirit, who is life, responded to the words of a young Jewish girl. He made it possible for her to become the mother of a baby who is God.

How beautiful Mary was! Her life became centered on the baby whom she would bring into the world.

At the moment of the angel's visit Mary seemed to hear voices in her house. It was the baby's life singing to her in her womb. If anyone else had known Mary's secret, they might have said, "You are the glory of Jerusalem, you are the joy of Israel. You are the woman who is honoring and saving our people."

Mary would have shaken her head, "No!" Such praise was for someone like Judith, the woman who had saved Bethulia. Instead she, Mary, knew that she hadn't done anything like that. She was only God's servant. She had given God her heart and her body so he could work his mystery in her.

She knelt down on the ground to adore God.

Joseph found her just like that when he came to join her in evening prayer. Joseph didn't know what to think.

Finally, Mary lifted her face to him. She looked as if she was returning from a faraway place.... She smiled but she couldn't speak. What was happening in her was God's mystery, and she wanted to guard it. That evening Mary's prayer was a great act of love for the baby who was living inside her.

Mary Visits Elizabeth

In the days following Gabriel's visit, Mary thought about the words she had heard. She thought about the greeting that told her of God's love for her. She thought about the announcement that she would give birth to the son of God. She thought about the throne that was promised to the baby.

Now, maybe, the events which led up to her engagement to Joseph made some sense. Joseph was one of David's descendants. She also remembered that Elizabeth, although she was elderly, was going to have a baby boy.

Mary felt that her place at that moment was with her cousin Elizabeth, who would need her help. So she decided to visit her. Mary spoke to Joseph about this, then took the first caravan going down to Judea. Mary might have even visited the Temple. Then she hurried to reach Ain Karim, in the mountains of Judea.

As Mary came to the house and joyfully greeted her cousin, Elizabeth felt the baby kicking inside her. She exclaimed, "Blessed are you among women, and blessed is the fruit of your womb. You believed that the Lord would keep his promise. Blessed are you, Mary."

They hugged each other like the closest of sisters.

Mary was overjoyed. The spirit of the prophets had revealed to Elizabeth the mystery which was being fulfilled inside of Mary. Mary sang:

My soul glorifies the Lord
and I rejoice in God, my savior.
For he has watched over me with love
though I am only small and poor.
Because of this men and women
forever will love me.
The almighty God, he who is holy,
has caused great things to happen in me.
His mercy is for everyone who

loves him.
Over the years he has done marvelous things.
He overthrew oppressors and lifted up the humble.
He has given food to the hungry
and has sent away the rich with empty hands.
He has rescued the people of Israel, his servants,
offering them his mercy
which he promised to Abraham and to his descendants, forever.

Then Zachary, Elizabeth's husband, came. He had happiness written all over his face, but he couldn't express it. He remained unable to speak because he had doubted that God would give him the son he had prayed so much for. And now, the child was about to be born.

So Mary shared in Elizabeth's joy. Together they praised God who doesn't abandon those who trust in him. Together they prepared the swaddling clothes for their babies. They had no secrets between them, since the Spirit had revealed God's mystery to them.

The three months passed quickly and Elizabeth had a son. Eight days later it was time to name him. The neighbors wanted to name him Zachary, after his father.

"No, no!" said Elizabeth, "he must be called John."

No one wanted to listen to her. Then Zachary made them give him a writing tablet. He wrote, "John is his name." God wanted the baby to be named John. At that moment Zachary was able to speak again. He praised God, saying:

Blessed is the Lord of Israel, our God
because he visited and saved his people.
He has given life to a powerful savior
from the house of David,

as he promised through the prophets.
And you, little one,
will be the prophet of the Almighty,
because you will go ahead of him.
You will go before him to prepare the people
to receive the salvation
of our merciful God.
God will send us his divine light
which will shine on those who are in the dark.
It will guide our steps down paths of love and peace.

Zachary felt that he had been pardoned for his lack of faith. He bent over baby John and kissed him.

Mary stayed close to Elizabeth for as long as Elizabeth needed her help. When they finally said good-bye, they all hoped for another happy gathering. There would be another meeting between the families, but it would be between the two sons. It would take place in another thirty or so years.

Mary, Joseph's Bride

Joseph was so happy to see Mary again that he hugged her. He took her to see the house, which was almost ready.

Mary was already showing signs of the baby she was carrying. When Joseph noticed this, he couldn't understand what had happened. Mary saw the confusion and doubt on Joseph's face. She wanted to comfort him and explain to him that the baby was going to be the Son of God. But she didn't know how. Why would Joseph believe such an unusual story?

Mary was sure that God himself would send his light into Joseph's heart.

She prayed:
Oh Lord, I entrust myself into your hands
for you love me.
Come to help us,

you who are the hope of your people.

Joseph suffered because he didn't know what to do. He didn't want to hurt Mary, who was so good. He also prayed and said:

God of Israel, you know my heart.

I'm trying so hard to follow the path you've chosen.

I beg you to free me from this sorrow,

and glorify your holy name.

One night, Joseph heard a voice in his sleep. "Joseph, son of David, don't be afraid to take Mary as your wife. The child growing within her comes from the Holy Spirit. Mary will have a baby boy and you will call him Jesus. He will save his people from their sins."

When he woke up, Joseph felt he was sharing in the mystery God was working in Mary. He understood that he had to take special care of her.

Their house was almost ready. As soon as it was finished, they could be married. When the baby arrived, Joseph would give him his family name.

Joseph quickly went to tell Mary that he had decided to celebrate their wedding as soon as possible. Mary listened and looked into his eyes. She saw that he no longer doubted. Had God's light reached Joseph, too? Did he understand? Mary believed this. Mary said to him, "Yes, Joseph. Get everything ready for the wedding. I will be your bride, but you know now that only God is my Lord. I belong to him."

The wedding day came. Mary wore the new slip, robe and veil, and the jewels which Joseph had given her when they were engaged. They received the blessing of their relatives. Then, as their friends and families celebrated, Mary was taken into Joseph's house where her new life began.

Joseph worked right outside the house. Every so often he would face the room where Mary was knitting peacefully. He would stop working to drink the cup of water she brought him. He would tell Mary not to tire herself out, and would watch her turn to put away the jug of fresh water. Then Joseph would return to work. He thought about what Mary had told him the day she agreed to celebrate their wedding: "I will be your wife, but you know that God is my only Lord."

He had understood this even before that day, because of the message he received in his dream. In his heart Joseph honored and greatly respected Mary, that young woman who hid the greatest mystery behind her simplicity. Joseph agreed to stay by her side as a brother, as the foster father of Mary's son.

Mary, Jesus' Mother

When the Roman emperor ordered something, you had to obey. So Mary and Joseph had to go to Bethlehem to sign their names in the city registers. Caesar Augustus wanted to know how many subjects he had in the vast Roman Empire.

Joseph would have liked to spare Mary that trip. But she said that she was fine, and that the baby was peaceful. If the Lord wanted it so, it was for the best. Accompanied by Joseph, Mary once again traveled the road that had brought her to Jerusalem. From there they reached Bethlehem, the city of David. David's descendants had gathered there from all over the country. The town was as packed as a...can of sardines.

Joseph searched for a place to stay with his relatives, but they all had guests. They said to him: "Here you won't even find a corner to curl up in. But down there, there's a cave where you can rest quietly."

Mary was worn out from the long trip, and every so often she grew weak.

A woman said to Joseph: "Brother, go quickly. Your wife needs to rest. And you, sister, be strong. I will come to see you shortly."

Joseph looked at Mary. She was calm and she was smiling at him, but her eyes seemed so big. He stopped searching for a room and,

holding Mary up, he reached the cave. There he re-lit the lantern, collected the clean, dry hay and made a cushion out of it for Mary to sleep on. He then helped Mary lie down, and made a fire to keep her warm.

It was so beautiful! Mary seemed to be full of light. A soft cry rang in the silence, then a wail. Mary smiled and whispered softly, "God is born!"

When Mary recovered, she found that the baby had been taken care of by the woman who had promised to come help her. Mary took the baby in her arms. She kissed him, and wanted Joseph to kiss him too. Then she wrapped him in swaddling clothes and put him in the manger, on the soft lambskin that the woman had brought.

"Everything is fine, Mary," the woman reassured her. "I brought you some bread and milk. Drink something; it will give you strength."

Mary thanked her and offered some to Joseph. He was sitting next to the manger and couldn't take his eyes off the baby. He could almost hear the words of one of the Lord's prophets:

And you, Bethlehem, in the land of Judah,
you are not really the smallest of the capitals of Judah.
From you will come the leader who will shepherd my people, the people of Israel.

Was the prophet speaking about this baby? Yes, the Lord had wanted this trip to Bethlehem so that the baby would be registered as one of David's descendants.

The woman was looking at Mary's lovely face and at the beautiful face of the newborn child. *Certainly,* she thought, *the little one takes after his mother.*

The woman said, "God is with you, my sister. May he make you a happy mother."

"Yes, the holy One has done great things in me," Mary answered.

"As soon as possible, we will make a place for you in our house. I'll come to see you in a little while."

"Thank you," Joseph murmured. They were the first words he was able to speak after the birth of the baby.

While the woman was walking away, Mary went near the manger. She knelt down next to Joseph. They prayed together and praised God for sending the Savior into the world.

I would have liked to have been there right next to Mary. I would have liked to ask her what she felt in her heart when she looked at her baby. I can almost hear her say, "He is my son. He is a baby different from every other baby in the world because he is God. But I am his mother and a mother is always the servant of her children. She is a servant of love. I am the mother of God because he was pleased with my littleness. I will continue to be a servant who loves God."

Mary and the Shepherds

Outside the cave some people were calling out from one place to another. The voices got softer, and then louder again.... Finally Joseph managed to understand their words:

"There is no one here," said a man's voice.

"Look up ahead," answered a woman's voice.

"Here is a cave all lit up."

By this time the people had reached the opening of the cave. Joseph rushed over to see who they were. They asked him, "Is there by chance a baby here?"

"Yes," Joseph answered, "he was just born."

"Perhaps he's the one we're looking for.... Don't be afraid, we're shepherds; we received a message and we were given a sign. May we come in?"

"Yes, of course. Wait one minute."

And Joseph went to tell Mary that they had visitors.

Mary had finished nursing the baby. She had just put him down in the manger to protect him from the cold.

"Let them come in," Mary said kindly. "They are poor like us. God loves them."

First a woman entered. She approached the manger and looked at the baby very closely.

"When was he born, sister?" she asked.

"This evening. He is my son," Mary replied.

The woman returned to the others and said, "The sign is here: a baby wrapped in swaddling clothes and lying in a manger."

"It is he! It is he!" the shepherds exclaimed all together. And they approached the manger.

"Show us your baby, please," they asked Mary.

Mary lifted up her son, smoothed back the lamb's wool from his face and showed him to the shepherds.

The woman took him in her arms and kissed him. "He's as beautiful as an angel," she sighed. She couldn't say anything else.

The shepherds wanted to take turns holding him close to their hearts. Even Mark, a young shepherd boy who had stayed with his father during the night-watch of the flock, wanted to kiss him. But he felt unworthy.

"Take him in your arms; he loves you," Mary assured him. And Mark kissed Jesus and hugged him as if he were his little brother.

"You must excuse us," one of the older men said. "While we were watching over our flock, we saw an angel surrounded by light. The angel said to us: 'Don't be afraid. I bring you news which will fill you with joy. Today in the city of David the Savior is born. He is the Lord Christ.'"

Daniel interrupted, "Perhaps because the angel saw that we were uncertain, he added, 'This is the sign: you will find the baby wrapped in swaddling clothes and lying in a manger.'"

"Yes," nodded Mark, "and there were many angels in the sky singing, 'Glory to God in the highest heaven and peace on earth to those whom God loves.'"

"We were given the sign," the elderly man continued, "and we immediately set out to look for the baby. And we've found him!"

"Blessed be our God, who has remembered us!" the shepherds exclaimed together.

Mary took the baby back from Mark's arms and praised God.

"I praise you, our God! You come to us in this baby to show your love and mercy toward the people of Israel."

The sun peeked through the mountains of Judea. Mary turned the baby toward the east and prayed. "Lord our God, your name is known throughout the world. We praise you because today you give us your light which comes to shine on those who live in the shadow of death. Jesus is our light; Jesus is our peace."

She gently wrapped her son in the lamb's wool and placed him back in the manger.

The shepherds were filled with a joy they couldn't keep to themselves. Although they were made fun of because they were poor, God had still chosen to give the sign to them. Now they knew that God loved them just the same. He had announced to them, before anyone else, that the Savior was born.

The shepherds left the cave and returned to their flocks. They told everyone they met the story of what they had seen and what the angel and the baby's mother had told them.

You may find it hard to believe, but the shepherds of Israel didn't know how to read or write. They weren't exactly saints either. But do you know what they became? God made them the first followers of his Son, and his first missionaries. They had searched for the baby and found him. They had seen him with their own eyes, but more importantly, they had seen him with their hearts. They accepted him as a friend. Even though he hadn't spoken, they listened to what Mary said about him.

You might say that the shepherds experienced God.

This seems like something very great and difficult to do. But the shepherds, in all of their littleness, found themselves very, very close to God.

Sometimes you and I can experience God too. When we do, we become Jesus' missionaries, because we can't keep the joy and the light of Jesus only for ourselves.

We should prepare our hearts to welcome Jesus every day, to speak heart to heart with him. How many things we could then learn about him! How many things we would be able to tell him, not only with our words, but also with our lives!

At dawn, Mary took a nap. Joseph sat down next to the baby, tenderly leaning over him. He was happy!

Jesus, the God Who Saves

Eight days later, many shepherds and local people gathered around the cave. The people in this crowd had come during the week, either one at a time or in groups, to see the baby. They were there because they somehow felt invited to the name-giving ceremony. They also wanted to congratulate the father and celebrate with the young mother who was not from their town.

The shepherds didn't know the baby's name. Mary and Joseph, however, had known it for months because the angel had told them. Mary's son would have a name that described his mission.

Joseph and Mary had spoken about it while they were waiting for the baby to be born.

"Joseph, do you remember the old prophecy about the 'suffering servant'? Do you think it spoke of our baby?" Mary had asked.

"God will let us know," Joseph had answered. "The prophet Isaiah said that the Lord's servant would suffer greatly, and then have many followers. He said that this man would carry on his shoulders the sins of many people."

That morning Joseph was thinking about the talks he had had with Mary in their little house in Nazareth. Then he realized that the shepherds had already arrived for the ceremony. He went out to thank them for coming to share in the celebration. Then the brief ceremony began. Joseph took the baby and held him high in the air. He slowly walked him in a circle, as if he wanted the little one to see everything around him: the people, the earth, the universe. Joseph stopped in front of the shepherds and said: "Jesus is his name."

There was a deep silence, as if they were awaiting a great event. Then a small boy exclaimed: "Jesus, the God who saves!" And he started to clap his hands with all his might.

Everyone repeated his name to the beat of the boy's clapping hands. And there was a great party in honor of Jesus, Mary and Joseph.

Forty days after Jesus' birth, Mary and Joseph took him to Jerusalem. They went to fulfill the two important requirements of the Jewish law: the purification of the mother and the presentation of the firstborn to the Lord.

They went up to the Temple. In the front hall Joseph bought two turtledoves, which were the offering of the poor. Then they went to the women's hall. Mary crossed the entrance and carried the two turtledoves to the priest. He offered one of them to thank the Lord for the child he had given Mary and Joseph. The other was offered as a sacrifice for forgiveness.

We know that the Lord loved Mary and that she was full of grace, just as the angel had said. She didn't need purification, but she wanted to obey the law as any other woman would.

Next Joseph and Mary presented the baby to the Lord. They came together and prayed. They were grateful for the gift which God had given to his people: his Son, the Savior. They knew that they were among the few who could thank God for this, because not many people had seen Jesus.

Then the little family turned to leave and begin their journey back to Bethlehem. Suddenly a man approached them from one of the Temple entrances. The Holy Spirit had told him that before he died, he would see the Messiah. The man's name was Simeon. He came up to Mary and held out his arms to the child. Then he held Jesus up, and praised God saying, "Lord, allow me to go in peace. Your servant's eyes have seen the Savior. They have seen the one whom you have sent for all people, to be their light and the glory of your people Israel."

Simeon had waited a lifetime to see this child. He had gently held all of the babies he had seen before Jesus. Each time that he had done so, the Holy Spirit had told him, "This is not the child." But in front of Mary's baby he heard the Holy Spirit say, "This is the one!"

He turned to Jesus and Mary and blessed them. Then he looked at Mary like someone who was reading an ancient scroll and trying to understand its meaning.

He slowly said, "This son will bring ruin or resurrection for many Israelites. He will be a sign from God which many people will reject. He will make people's thoughts clear. And you, his mother, your heart will be pierced by sorrow and pain as sharp as a sword."

Mary cried. She took her son back into her arms and held him close to her heart. And there, in the presence of the Lord of the Temple, she promised to remain by Jesus' side. She promised to share in his suffering, to comfort him, to love him for those who would not love him.

That was not the only time that day that Joseph and Mary were shocked by the things they heard about Jesus. Although Jesus was still so small, the Spirit was already revealing him to the people. In fact, even Ann, an elderly prophetess, had come to the Temple at that moment. She thanked God for the baby. She spoke about him to everyone she met, and to everyone who was waiting for the Savior.

We don't know if Ann knew Mary and had seen her as a little girl. But at that moment she said what God told her to say.

Wherever Mary goes, Jesus goes with her. The Spirit of the Lord also goes there. The Holy Spirit opens the minds and hearts of people. He helps them understand and love Jesus, their Savior.

People gathered excitedly around the little family. Mary and Joseph tried to protect the baby from the curiosity of the crowd. God his Father would reveal who Jesus was.

Holding her son close to her, Mary set out with Joseph toward Bethlehem.

The Three Wise Men Arrive

Let's catch up with Mary and Joseph and head back to Bethlehem with them.

Mary handled the long trip well. Jesus was the least tired. He had spent the journey in either Mary's or Joseph's arms, and had eaten and slept wonderfully.

When they reached the first houses of Bethlehem, some young children were waiting to welcome them. They already felt friendly toward Jesus. And the woman who had taken care of Mary and baby Jesus on that first night was also waiting for them.

"Welcome back! We're so happy to have you with us again!"

"Thank you," Joseph and Mary replied. "We've come home."

"Yes, Mary, that's right. Now that you've taken care of your duty, you're free to go wherever you want. You can come live in the house we've prepared for you. It's very plain, like all of our houses, but it's warmer and more comfortable than the cave."

"You are so good to us," Joseph said. "God will bless you."

The neighbor woman led the way to the new house. Joseph found that it was certainly better than the cave, especially for the baby. Mary looked around and discovered that a cradle had already been placed in the best corner. It was made of an old yet strong cloth hung from two posts that were firmly planted in the ground. Who knows, maybe Joseph had something else in mind for the baby.... But there was plenty of time to take care of that.

The woman placed Jesus in the cradle and went to light the fire. Mary was touched because the neighbors had even left them some bread, milk, figs, olives and oil. There was also some water for them. Joseph's relatives had provided everything they needed. In their hearts Mary and Joseph knew that God was watching over his son.

When they were alone, Mary and Joseph sat down to catch their breath. They would have plenty of time later on to worry

about settling in. They would also need to arrange their simple belongings and the things they had collected for the baby.

So the family had a home of its own. Joseph found a job with one of his relatives. He worked with great energy, as if it were his own carpentry shop. But he wanted so badly to be with Mary and the baby that the hours seemed very long.

People would ask him, "Joseph, how's your baby boy? Is he getting big?"

Jesus wasn't truly his son, but Joseph loved him as if he were his own flesh and blood. And he worked hard so that Mary and Jesus would have everything they needed.

In the evening Mary would greet him kindly. "Peace be with you, Joseph."

"Peace be with you, Mary," Joseph would answer. And he would ask her how she was feeling, if she needed anything, if she wanted him to go and get some water from the fountain, if Jesus had eaten and taken his nap…. Joseph would stay close by the cradle. He would take Jesus in his strong arms and gently hug him. He would speak to him for a long time, using strange words which aren't found in any dictionary. Jesus would open his eyes wide and reach out with his little hands. Joseph would tickle him to make him smile, and that smile made Joseph happy.

One day Joseph asked the man who had given him the job, "Could I take the day off tomorrow? I have a few things to take care of."

His kind boss said yes. So Joseph spent the day at home. He wanted to rearrange the crib so that it would be easier for Mary to take care of the baby.

He had already woven a basket out of reeds. They were strong and wide so that the baby could move around freely. He had also woven together several strips of sheepskin leather to use as cords. That day Joseph wanted to strengthen the beams of the roof so he could hang the reed basket from them.

Mary helped him. She handed him a nail or the hammer. She pulled the cord, and gave Joseph advice about how high to hang the basket. When everything was ready, Mary came in and placed her little bundle in the cradle, rocking it gently.

Baby Jesus laughed and Mary and Joseph laughed with him. Jesus was really the joy of their lives.

Months passed by.... One late afternoon Mary and Joseph heard several voices and the pounding of hooves. Joseph listened closely and could only tell that the strangers were foreigners.

"They must be lost. I'll go see," Joseph said. Joseph opened the door. Mary followed him.

They saw the humped backs of three camels and people wearing strange clothing. The people were looking above the house and pointing at something up in the sky.

Joseph went out and also looked above the house. High in the sky there was a star which seemed to be directly over the house. Joseph motioned to Mary, who also came out. She saw the star then went back into the house, smiling in wonder.

At that moment three men stepped away from the group. They came toward the doorway where Joseph was standing.

One of them asked, "Is the King of the Jews, who was just born, here? We asked Herod, but he denied that any king was born. He sent us on our way. He said that if we found the king, we should let him know."

"Yes," continued a handsome black man, "he must have been born in this area. We saw his star rise in the sky and we have come to adore him."

"The Scribes of Bethlehem have examined your Scriptures. They told us that the king will come from Bethlehem," the third man explained. "And, look! The star which we have followed from our own countries in the east is shining directly over your house."

Joseph didn't know what to say. He moved aside and let them enter. Inside the house they found the baby. Mary was holding him in her arms.

The three wise men bowed down and adored Jesus.

The angel had told Mary that God would give the throne of King David to the baby, but no one knew just what those words meant. These men, who knew the movements of the stars, had noticed a special star. They realized that it had to be the one the Jewish people were waiting for. In their holy books was written: "A star will come from Jacob, and a scepter will rise out of Israel." The wise men had decided to follow the star, which guided them—not to Jerusalem, where Herod was ruling—but to Bethlehem where there was no king.

But the king had to be there, since his star had led the way! It was the Holy Spirit who was telling the wise men about the presence of the King of the Jews.

Mary let the wise men bow before the baby as she held him on her lap. Then she lifted him in the air. Jesus moved his little hands as if he were blessing them.

The wise men rose. They opened their treasures, and offered gifts of gold, incense and myrrh to the baby. These gifts were the riches of their land. They were a sign of the wise men's faith in the baby.

The gifts surprised Mary and Joseph, mostly because of what they stood for. Mary's eyes grew sad because she knew the myrrh was a symbol of the suffering

Simeon had talked about. Then she motioned to Joseph and he brought her some bread. Mary put it in Jesus' hands and told him to give it to the men. She said, "May this bread of Bethlehem give you strength for your journey. Shalom!"

"Shalom," the wise men answered. They were deeply moved, and their eyes shone with great joy.

Night had already fallen and the star was shining. The wise men lay down to rest, but several hours later they were already up to begin their journey. An angel had warned them in their dreams not to return to Herod. And so they started their journey home down a different road than the one which had led them to Jesus.

We Must Save the Baby!

The wise men had just left when an angel appeared to Joseph in a dream and said, "Get up and take the baby and his mother and flee to Egypt. Stay there until I let you know that it's safe. Herod is looking for the baby and he wants to kill him!"

Joseph roused himself from his sleep. He tried to stay calm and then called, "Mary! Mary!"

"Yes, Joseph. What is it?"

"We must save the baby! Herod is searching for him and he wants to have him killed."

"We must have faith in the Lord. He will take care of his son and guide us," Mary answered.

"The Lord is leading us to Egypt, but we must hurry," urged Joseph.

Mary didn't ask any questions. This time she learned the will of God through Joseph and she willingly obeyed.

Joseph collected in a goatskin cloth all the things he wanted to bring: two robes, things for the journey, and the gifts received from the wise men. Mary gathered up the baby's clothes and a little robe given to him for his birthday. They wrapped everything in a bundle and placed it on Joseph's back. Joseph then added oil to the lantern. He helped Mary to bundle up Jesus, who didn't even wake up.

"As soon as we can, we'll buy a donkey so that we can escape more quickly," Joseph promised.

Outside there was a deep silence. The moon appeared and disappeared behind the clouds.

"And the wise men? Where are they?" Mary asked.

"They have already broken camp and are probably far away by now."

"May the Lord our God guide us."

"Let's go, Mary! We go in the name of God. Be strong!"

Mary held Jesus to her heart and began to pray, "Lord you are my shepherd. Even if I pass through a dark valley, I will not fear. You are with me and you keep me safe."

Mary started to cry. Why did they want to kill her baby? He hadn't harmed anyone. He was their Savior.

The little family moved on, trying not to make any noise. Herod's soldiers might jump out from any street, woods or vineyard. Mary and Joseph knew of Herod's cruelty. They knew that he would do anything to get rid of the baby.

Mary and Joseph felt responsible for Jesus' life, and they walked quickly. A little before dawn they heard a cart coming. They were frightened. When it came closer, the man who was driving called out to them in a friendly way, "Peace be with you, friends. Are you going far? Would you like a ride?"

Mary and Joseph looked at each other and agreed that it seemed safe.

"Thank you, brother. We'll gladly accept a ride," Joseph answered the man.

Joseph made a space for Mary to lie down in the cart. He laid Jesus next to her and covered them with his cloak. He could do without it.

"Did you know," said the farmer, "that all of Jerusalem is up in arms?"

"Why, brother?" Joseph asked.

"Because certain wise men came from the east and wanted to speak to Herod. And do you know what they were looking for? The newborn King of the Jews."

"And did they find him?"

"Are you kidding? Herod already has enough children, don't you think?"

"Yes, I definitely agree," Joseph answered convincingly.

"Herod has given our beautiful Temple back to us. But he holds all of the citizens under the point of his sword, even his children and his wives," said the farmer.

"The God of Israel will have mercy on us and he will send us the Messiah," Joseph said. He didn't want to upset Mary with such talk. But meanwhile his heart was aching because he knew that this time his son Jesus was threatened by Herod's sword.

(By this time Joseph was used to saying: "my son, my little boy".... Mary was always happy when she heard him talk about Jesus like this.)

As soon as the sun began to rise, Joseph decided that it was not safe to continue traveling so visibly.

"Well, brother, we'll get off here and be on our way," Joseph told the farmer. "Thank you very much. You've been a great help to us."

"Well, you know, having a little traveling company is always a pleasure. Until we meet again!"

"Thank you and peace be with you, brother."

Joseph and Mary stepped down and picked up their bundles. The farmer waved to them and spurred on his donkey.

Joseph remembered that the farmer had not said anything about Herod's search for the baby. Maybe they had a slight advantage over their persecutor. Still, when they reached the first small marketplace, Joseph bought a young donkey to make Mary's trip more comfortable. It would also help them to speed up their journey to safety. And so they continued toward Egypt, using the less traveled roads and making only brief stops.

Together they went down to Egypt, the ancient land where the Jewish slaves had toiled. This was the land that had been punished by God with the natural disasters of the frogs, the locusts and the bad water. The Egyptians had also been punished with the death of the firstborn boys, including the pharaoh's son. God did this in order to set his people free.

Joseph said aloud, "God truly guides the history of his people according to his plans. Here we are, and our old enemies now accept us. They offer us work and a way to make a living."

"We'll find other Jewish people, won't we Joseph?" Mary asked.

"I think so. We will look for a Jewish community close to the border. We'll wait until God tells us that it is safe to go back."

Once again Mary received the instructions given by the Lord through Joseph. She accepted them.

They were just about to reach the last guard tower. On the other side was Egypt, and the baby was saved!

We can understand how relieved Mary and Joseph must have been when they passed the final tower. With their fears calmed, they must have cried with joy. Herod could no longer hurt Jesus.

Mary in Egypt

During this time, Mary and Joseph hadn't met any caravans coming from their homeland. But, as soon as they entered Egyptian territory, they noticed some merchants camped out with their camels near a small well. The camels immediately attracted Jesus' attention. Joseph kept Jesus in his arms because he was getting excited. He took him over to where the animals were lying and let Jesus down to pet some of them.

Mary came up beside them. She was a little worried. A merchant started speaking to them and soon realized that Joseph couldn't understand. So he repeated his words in Aramaic.

"You're Jewish, right? I can tell by your robe."

"Yes," Joseph answered, "we are Jewish."

"You're lucky, because if you were in Bethlehem your baby would be under Herod's sword. He has ordered all the children from one to two-years-old to be killed. He believes that one of them was born to be king."

Mary and Joseph pulled Jesus close to them.

"Don't worry," said the stranger, "Herod is far away. Come on, put this nice little boy on the back of my camel. He'll have fun."

In fact, as soon as he was on the camel, Jesus clapped his hands with joy. Joseph said, "He even feels at home up there!"

"You're right," Mary sighed. But Jesus' joy couldn't take away the pain she was feeling for all of the mothers in Bethlehem who were crying for their babies. She knew some babies of that age in Bethlehem.

Mary shook her head sadly. "Poor Sarah, who knows if she was able to save her baby?"

"And I wonder if Joanna was able to hide her son? He certainly isn't more than two years old," Joseph added.

"God has saved our baby," Mary said as she watched the merchant carry Jesus down from the camel. "He tests us with suffering but he doesn't leave us. He is here with us."

We know that merchants in those days wandered from one country to another selling gold, spices, perfumes, fabric.... But you certainly must have figured out that they had another important job. In those days they were the newspaper, the television and the radio. They spread the news. It was because of their information

that Joseph came to believe it was time to head farther into Egypt. So Joseph, Mary and Jesus traveled on and stopped in a Jewish community farther inland. There they found hospitality and work for Joseph.

Jewish people knew that wherever they went, they could count on their fellow Jews. Giving shelter to a traveler or foreigner was considered a sacred duty. In fact, the Jewish people really understood the suffering of refugees. They had been refugees themselves in Egypt, Syria, and Babylon....

So, while Joseph worked with another Jewish carpenter, Mary took care of Jesus. She helped him get acquainted with the other children. She took care of the elderly and the sick people in the neighborhood. The people came to love Mary, who was always eager to do an act of charity for anyone in need. She inspired confidence in the God of Israel. She kept her son close by, looking after him as if he were a rare pearl. Baby Jesus was a little different from the others, but no one quite knew why. Was it the light that would suddenly shine in his eyes? Was it the smile that came to his face when he saw an act of kindness? Who knew? There was just something different about Mary's son. The other mothers thought, "Maybe she realizes that her son is special." Mary treated her son with the same respect the rabbi had for the holy scrolls of the Bible.

Jesus is the Word of the Father. Jesus is the one whom the Bible prepared the way for. How could Mary not have great respect for him?

A year passed, and then another, and yet another. Mary and Joseph watched Jesus grow up right before their eyes. Every so often he needed a longer robe or new sandals. He would run around a lot, and his little feet were growing. He learned many

Egyptian words and he would repeat them to his father when he came home at night. Jesus picked up the language very quickly, and would tell strange parables full of wisdom.

"As soon as he's six years old we'll put him in the rabbi's school," Joseph said.

"I agree. He should start right away. We don't know how much longer we'll be staying here," Mary answered.

And it's true, neither Mary nor Joseph knew how long they would stay in that little corner of Egypt. God knew, however.

Joseph went to the synagogue with Mary and listened to the reading from the prophets. He understood that the hour of Israel's liberation was near. At home he would speak with Mary about this. Jesus would listen and nod his head in agreement.

In the meantime, Mary and Joseph were busy teaching Jesus about the history of his people. Joseph would say: "God acts toward Israel as a mother eagle acts toward her young. When she wants them to learn how to fly, do you know what she does? She jumps from the nest with her wings spread. She flies in sweeping circles around the nest so that the young ones will see. Then she goes back to the nest. She stays with them for a little while and then...once again, she is out of the nest and flying in the clear sky. When she goes back she says: 'Who is coming with me?' 'Me! Me!' say the little ones. 'Okay, you can come today.' The eagle takes flight and goes right under the nest. Each baby eagle jumps on the wings of the mother and flies with her. Then he tries a small flight alone and the mother comes around to take him back on her wings. They do this until the little one gains his courage. He flies, flies, flies far off into the deep blue sky, very happy.... There you see, God is to us like the mother eagle is to her young."

"That's great!" exclaimed Jesus. "God loves Israel. He takes his people on his wings so that they will learn to fly, to live. And Israel learned, right, Father?"

Joseph would answer Jesus' questions. He happily spent the Lord's holy day of rest together with Jesus and Mary. And he would tell of the many ways in which God showed his love for Israel.

"Sometimes the people would worship idols. Have you ever seen the Egyptian idols?"

"Yes, I saw Miriam's small idols. I know that her family worships the sun. The sun was created by my Father in heaven."

Jesus stopped speaking. He felt that he had said too much.

Joseph waited a moment. Then he said, "We want to always remember that the Lord is our only God. Tonight let's remember together the great commandment he gave us."

Joseph began and then Mary and Jesus joined in:
Listen Israel, about the Lord, who is our God, our one and only God.
You will love the Lord your God with all of your heart,
with all of your soul
and with all of your strength.
And together they praised God:
Praise the Lord from the heavens!
Praise him way up in the high heavens.
Praise him, you his angels.
Praise him, all ranks of angels.
Praise him, sun and moon.
Praise him, heavens on high, you, the waters over the heavens.
May everyone praise the name of the Lord
for he said the word and everything was created.
His name is great,
his glory shines
on the earth and in the heavens.

He has given strength to his people.

Time was passing. One day a caravan of merchants came along and stopped at the town well. There were many children around the caravan, and Jesus wanted to mount a camel.

One of the merchants recognized him: "You still like to play caravan leader, huh? Even now that you've gotten bigger?"

"Yes, I would like to ride in the silence, in the desert, to look at the stars and to think about God."

"You speak like the old prophets of your people. What will you do when you grow up?"

"I will dig the deepest of wells. Everyone will come to drink the water I will give them."

"Good boy, Jesus! When you begin working, call me! I want to work with you."

"I will need many hands to help. And it will be wonderful, believe me," Jesus answered him.

Mary was watching her son closely. "He's really growing up. I didn't even realize it," she thought.

Joseph came up to her and whispered, "Have you heard? Herod is dead. The merchants are talking about it."

Mary, who had been deep in thought about her son, was startled.

The desert "newspapers" had left their message. Mary and Joseph had to read it and try to find out what God wanted them to do.

"We'll keep waiting. God will send us a sign," Joseph said.

"Yes, we will wait," Mary answered.

One night Joseph heard the voice which he knew well.

"Get up!" it said. "Return to the land of Israel. Jesus' persecutors are dead."

Joseph told Mary about the Lord's command.

"We won't go back to Bethlehem, Mary. It seems that Archelaus, the new king, is not very different from his father. We will go back to Nazareth."

When Jesus, Mary and Joseph were ready to leave, many people gathered around Jesus. There were not only the boys his own age, but also the girls and the older children.

Their cries of "Shalom!" filled the air.

Mary in Jerusalem

Mary and Joseph were in Nazareth for five or six years. Although Jesus had come from Egypt, where many things were different, he easily got used to his new home. People called him the son of Mary or the son of the carpenter. They were happy that Joseph had chosen to bring his family to Nazareth instead of Bethlehem, the city of David. The young children who were Jesus' age all wanted Jesus to play with them. They wanted him to be on their teams. At that time there weren't any football games or tennis matches. But those children found ways of having fun and competing with one another. They competed in running, wrestling, high-jumping.... The children's robes flew everywhere and sometimes ended up in rags.

There were also contests that involved the intelligence and memory of the boys and girls. Some were about the history of God's people. At that time, there were neither books nor notebooks. The Jewish children's books were their memories. The contests tested the sharp memories of the young people, who remembered facts and names of important people and places.

These contests were very popular and everyone wanted to win first prize.

Jesus participated with all his heart. He didn't like to do things halfway.

Mary watched him grow strong, wise, and full of kindness. She rejoiced at seeing him grow to be a wonderful teenager with a serious way about him.

The great springtime holiday, Passover, was coming. Mary and Joseph discussed whether or not they should bring Jesus to Jerusalem.

"Yes, certainly," Mary said. "Last year Jesus wanted so badly to come with us, remember? We were convinced that the trip would be too much for him. This

year is different though. He is strong and healthy, and he can easily bear the cold weather. I really believe that the experience of Passsover in Jerusalem among so many Jews from all over the empire will be something special."

"I agree," answered Joseph.

Jesus was very happy with the idea.

"Certainly, Father, I have to come. I am strong and healthy. I can handle the trip without problems and help Mother. This Passover is important to me. Soon I will be one of the adults in the community, a real 'Son of God's Law.'"

So Mary and Joseph prepared everything necessary. They left for Jerusalem in a caravan with other people from Nazareth.

At mealtime, Jesus showed up to help prepare the food and to receive his portion. Then they would wait for Joseph to begin the blessing of the food.

"Blessed are you, our God, King of the universe, who gives us food from the earth."

This was their daily prayer, but it must have meant more to them during the pilgrimage to the Temple in Jerusalem.

You know, the pilgrimage was no vacation for an Israelite. It meant remembering and reliving their ancestors' long march across the desert to Sinai, where they met God before traveling on to the promised land.

After four days of praying and singing, the people of Nazareth arrived in the holy city. They looked for a place to stay with relatives, and got ready for the Passover holiday.

Jesus, however, wanted to go up to the Temple right away. He wanted to pray and to admire the beauty of the Lord's house. In the afternoon sun it must have looked like it was completely covered in gold. Some of Jesus' friends were with him.

Mary knew how important prayer was for her son. She gladly allowed him to go up to the Temple and to pray with the other Israelites. At that hour they would be offering the evening sacrifice. She said to him,

"Go, and may you remain in the presence of the Lord."

Upon returning, Jesus was very quiet. Mary watched him without letting him notice. "It's the first time that he has seen Jerusalem and the Temple. What could be on his mind?" she wondered. She didn't ask him any questions. Mary respected Jesus' times of silence. But before laying down on his mat to rest, Jesus kissed his mother and said, "Mother, the temple is right here!" And he pointed to himself.

Mary began to cry and her tears fell on Jesus' face.

During the night, Mary thought again about the words of the angel, "Your baby is the son of the Almighty." The body of Jesus was truly the temple where God was present and adored. She got up from bed, got down on her knees, and adored her son.

The next morning the pilgrims from Jerusalem went up to the Temple to pray and to offer the morning sacrifice of incense. They walked up the hill, singing:

What joy when they told me:
we will go to the Lord's house.
And now, we are here
at your front door, Jerusalem.

The women stopped in the courtyard reserved for them. The men continued until they reached the courtyard of Israel.

The priest came and entered the "holy of holies." While the Levites sang, the priest went up to the altar with the incense. He offered the sacrifice of the incense to the God of Israel.

Mary looked at Jesus who stood by her side. In her heart she prayed, "May God be adored and praised."

The word "sacrifice" reminded Mary about what Simeon had told her in that same Temple: that her baby would cause her great pain. Since the time of their suffering during the flight to Egypt, everything had gone well. What else would happen?

"God of Israel," she prayed, "I am your servant. I place myself in your hands. Do whatever you wish with me."

After the morning sacrifice, Joseph went to get Jesus. Together they began to prepare for the Passover. They bought the lamb and brought it to the priest who killed it and poured its blood on the altar. He burned the internal parts and gave Joseph the parts that he would use for the meal. Joseph brought them to the house of Mary's relatives, so that they could be roasted according to the Law.

Jesus began to understand that his Father was waiting for another sacrifice. The lamb of that sacrifice would be Jesus.

He thought of all this until after dark. In the evening everyone gathered together in the largest room of the house. It was already decorated for the Passover celebration.

Everyone put on their best robes. The women put precious jewels on their veils, necks, arms and ankles. A festive mood in the air lifted everyone's spirits. Jesus took part in it, and he sang with his soft voice which had not yet begun to change.

The celebrations lasted until midnight. They ended with words of blessing for all.

The next day was a day of rest, prayer and brotherhood. The relatives had planned the day for their guests.

For Jesus it was truly a new Passover. He felt that he had touched the people's faith in God.

Every Jew celebrated and rejoiced because God had freed every one of them.

Even Joseph and Mary seemed more carefree and happy. And Jesus was happy with them.

Son, Why Have You Done This?

Three days later they got ready to leave. Jesus helped Joseph and Mary fold up their mats and put them in a sack. He kindly said good-bye to his relatives. They paid him many compliments and wished him well.

Jesus replied, "Now I'm leaving, and I bet you know where I'm going. Don't worry, we will see each other again."

"He's going back up to the Temple to pray by himself," said Mary. She and Joseph stayed a little while longer with their relatives to thank them for their hospitality.

"Good-bye, Mary! Good-bye, Joseph!" interrupted little Martha. "Say good-bye to Jesus for me. Tell him that I'll be waiting for him next Passover. It's so great being with him. He knows so many stories about Judith, Samson, Samuel…. I know he'll tell me some more."

Joseph kissed her, Mary tenderly touched her face, and then they left.

The people were reuniting in the caravan. They sang one more song of praise to their Redeemer, who dwelt in the Temple. Soon the caravan leader began to move. Behind him the donkeys pulled carts overflowing with household items purchased in the bazaars of Jerusalem. Then there were the groups of men and groups of women. The children were running around the caravan.

Mary watched carefully until she saw a robe blowing in the distance.

"Jesus is back," she said to Joseph. Then they left peacefully, each in their own group.

As they walked, the travelers talked about the city and the number of people who had come to Jerusalem to celebrate. The men discussed the strict order that the Romans maintained. They talked about the beauty of the Temple and the gold decorations which were continually being added.

"Sure, it's all very beautiful, but who knows how long it will take us to pay for it!"

"Even so, it's becoming a marvelous sight which many people are envious of."

"And the Romans, when will they stop draining us with taxes? We need to do what the Maccabees did."

"Every so often some Israelites start to make waves, but...nothing ever comes of it. What can you expect just a few rebels to do?"

"It's time God started thinking more about our situation. Maybe he will send us another Moses."

Joseph was listening. Perhaps they already had another Moses. Yet Joseph knew that Jesus would never support an armed conflict. He stood for brotherhood and love.

At sundown, the leader gave the order to bed down the caravan. The families got together to prepare for the evening meal and night's rest. Joseph went to draw some water. Mary pulled some bread, figs and three hard-boiled eggs out of a sack. She looked around and tried to spot Jesus' robe, but she couldn't find him.

"Joseph, I can't find Jesus. Why hasn't he joined us?" she asked. Joseph heard fear in her voice and saw it in her eyes.

"I'll go look for him. You stay here and don't worry. Someone probably invited him for dinner."

Mary continued waiting and watching. By this time night was falling and she could no longer see anything in the darkness. The only thing she heard were the voices calling out: "Jesus! Jesus! Jesus!"

"Oh Lord, my God, look at me your servant. I beg you to send me my son, who is also yours...." And she cried.

When she saw Joseph return alone, her heart began to ache.

"You didn't find him, Joseph?"

"No one has seen him all day. Not even his friends Jude, Simon or Jonah, have seen him."

"Maybe he never left at all. Do you remember, while we were leaving, he said he was going.... Where was it?"

"Yes, but I don't remember where or with whom."

"Let's go back to Jerusalem!" Mary said firmly.

Joseph knew that even though Mary was tired, she wouldn't wait one minute. Her fear was stronger than her tiredness. With their hearts filled with worry, Mary and Joseph returned to Jerusalem in the dark.

"We'll find him, Mary. He's probably with our relatives. God wouldn't want to take him away from us at such a young age."

Joseph helped Mary through the more difficult parts of the trip. As she leaned on his arm, he felt her trembling.

They reached Jerusalem early in the morning, and went immediately to their relatives' house. "Why haven't you left yet? We figured that you'd just about be in Samaria by now."

"We can't find Jesus!" Mary said. Her voice was weak with emotion. She fell into her relative's arms to be comforted.

"Jesus isn't with you?"

"We must search for him here in the city because yesterday no one in the caravan saw him," replied Joseph.

"Rest for just a minute first, wash off your feet, then we'll all set out to look for him. Better yet..." and the woman went to call Dan, an older boy who had spent a lot of time with Jesus. She sent him to search the streets where the caravan had been.

Martha understood that Jesus was lost. With tears in her eyes she offered to go help Dan.

"You stay here," her brother said to her. "Comfort Mary. I'll bring Jesus back."

Joseph went to check all the streets which led to the Temple. He begged Mary to rest for a while. He knew that he was asking her to do something difficult for her, and he tried to give her courage.

"Be strong, Mary! We must have faith that nothing will happen to our boy. God is with him."

Mary was very worried, but she managed to smile. She wanted to say: "But he is God!" Instead she softly said, "Go, Joseph, and come back with God."

Usually when people parted they would say "Go with God." Instead Mary said, "come back with God." And Joseph understood....

By the afternoon both Dan and Joseph had come back. Jesus was nowhere to be found.

Later on Mary and Joseph went up to the Temple. Before the evening prayer they searched in every corner, every entranceway, all of the rooms surrounding the Temple. Nothing. Jesus wasn't there.

On the second day some other relatives and a few volunteers joined in the search, but they had no luck.

On the third day Mary wanted to go back up to the Temple to speak to God about her pain. It was even sharper than when they had fled to Egypt. She had suffered then, but at least she had Jesus with her. This time he wasn't there. A mother can lose everything, but not her child! Do you know why? Because her child is her life. When a mother loses her child, she loses a part of herself.

Mary humbly went to pray in the women's courtyard of the Temple. We don't know what she said to God about her son. After all, he was also God's son. Maybe Mary told God that it was his turn to watch over Jesus and to send him safely back home. Joseph was already doing all that he could.

The women who were close by overheard Mary softly crying. Suddenly they saw her dry her eyes with the edge of her cloak and bow down in the presence of the Lord. Then she went out.

"Come here!" Mary said to Joseph who was waiting for her in the courtyard. "Come here! Maybe..." and she pulled him towards the room where the teachers of the Law were lecturing. These teachers answered the questions of persons who wanted to listen and understand more about the Bible.

Mary walked forward and...her heart skipped a beat. She saw Jesus. She wanted to call out to him, but she had a knot in her throat. She pointed him out to Joseph. Jesus was seated among the teachers and was listening attentively. But he was also asking them questions. Mary didn't hear the question he asked. She realized, however, that the teachers were looking at him with astonishment and listening to him. The people around him admired the intelligence of the boy. They were amazed at the answers he gave and the questions he asked.

Mary and Joseph were surprised because Jesus was usually rather quiet.

Lovingly Mary said, "Son." In her voice there was a trace of the pain she felt. "Why have you behaved like this with us? Your father and I were so worried. We looked all over for you."

"Why did you have to look for me? You know that I have to be involved in the things that concern my Father."

They should have known? How? Maybe when he had gone out he had told them where he was going…. The two of them, busy preparing for the trip, hadn't understood where he was going or whom he was going to see.

Mary and Joseph didn't completely understand Jesus' words now, either. But they understood that he knew where he had come from. They realized that Jesus had many tasks to carry out for his true Father.

As if nothing had happened, Jesus got up and went with Mary and Joseph. Together they returned to Nazareth with the first caravan they found heading for Galilee.

Mary noticed that Jesus continued to be a very good son. He was obedient to her and to Joseph, just as we are with our parents.

We don't know if Mary and Joseph ever spoke again about this event. We do know that Mary remembered all the details of what happened, as she remembered so many other events in the life of Jesus.

Jesus' mother didn't have one of those beautiful journals with a pretty gold border. But she had her heart. Mary remembered events, conversations and the people who were a part of Jesus' life. She kept them in her heart and thought about them.

In those moments Mary was growing. She didn't know everything about Jesus. Like us, she needed time to let her faith grow. It's nice to know this so that we, too, can hope to grow each day. We can hope to have an inner beauty and grace like Mary's.

When Luke the evangelist asked Mary to tell him about Jesus, she opened up her "journal," that is, her heart. She read to him everything that she had written there. Luke dipped his pen in ink and wrote on parchment what Mary had written in her heart.

This is how we know all of these things about Jesus, the son of Mary.

Three Hearts in One

Jesus, Mary and Joseph lived like any other family in Nazareth. They didn't talk about the family's background as descendants of David. Mary and Joseph didn't discuss Jesus' miraculous birth. Meanwhile, Jesus was growing up and gaining great wisdom. Jesus was loved by the people and by God his Father.

Joseph would work in his shop and now and then Jesus would help out.

Jesus had prepared himself to become a "son of the Law." He learned from the rabbi of Nazareth how to read in Hebrew the words to be read in the synagogue. He studied with great joy and diligence. Jesus was like that. He put his whole heart into whatever he set out to do.

The Saturday following his thirteenth birthday Jesus went to the synagogue. There he read in Hebrew the words of the Law and of the Prophets. Everyone could see that the words he read were close to his heart. He paid close attention to the rabbi as he spoke. Jesus received the blessing that would be with him for his whole life.

May the Lord bless and protect you.
May the face of the Lord shine on you,
and may he look favorably upon you.
May the Lord turn his glance toward you
and grant you peace.

Joseph had seated himself in front of the reader's stand. He was watching Jesus very closely so as not to miss the slightest expression or word. And he prayed, "God, you have chosen me to stand in your place as Jesus' father. I am just a carpenter. You don't need me to do great deeds. You are the one who works wonders. I thank you for having placed me next to the Holy One. Place me next to him in your kingdom."

Mary had gone to the women's section. She felt the eyes of the other mothers turn from Jesus toward her. They whispered, "He

resembles her so much, like two peas in a pod."

"It's so beautiful to see," murmured Ruth.

Mary, smiling at Ruth, put her finger to her lips to signal her to be quiet. But even Mary looked at Jesus. She noticed that he looked more handsome than usual. Why did his face seem so full of light? Maybe the knowledge that he was the Savior of his people was growing inside of him. That was his mission; he was "the Lord-Jesus who saves."

But he was still a boy. Mary had sewn a special robe for him just for the occasion. It was one piece and white with a striped cape. It gave him the look of a rabbi.

That Saturday Jesus rested at home according to the Lord's commandment. The lunch, which was prepared especially to celebrate the "son of the Law," was ready. Joseph blessed the food. For the rest of the day it was Jesus who acted as the teacher. That day he felt like a true

Israelite. Mary and Joseph were the young rabbi's two students. He said things which his parents had never heard before, and they were amazed.

In the carpenter workshop, though, Joseph was the one who taught. Jesus continued to be a quick learner. Sometimes he liked to do things in a different way, but he talked about it with his father first.

Two years, then three, then four passed by. Jesus was becoming a fine young man. Every girl in Nazareth looked at him with the secret hope of being chosen as his bride.

Naomi would tell her friends how she felt: "He's handsome, honest, intelligent and respectful. He has a trade, but sometimes he gets on my nerves. Why is he always so serious? Do you think he'll choose his bride from the young women of Cana or of Sepphoris?"

"Something tells me he'll never get married," Ruth would interrupt. "I think this every time I see him in the synagogue. He sits there next to Joseph, but you can clearly see that his mind is far off. He will become a prophet."

The other young women would get angry when Ruth talked like that. She lessened their hopes. Sometimes they would come to Mary with some excuse: an embroidery stitch to learn, a small cut which needed to be treated, something to show to Joseph. They would remain there with their eyes on Jesus. He would greet them and then continue hammering, planing, or measuring boards.

Mary understood why the girls visited. She would very carefully help them understand that the paths of men could lead in many different directions. It is impossible to tell what path a man would choose.

"One path can lead to a family with many children. Another could extend far away and lead to the salvation of many people. I don't know which path my son will follow. I think it will be a long one that will take him far away," Mary would say.

The young women would turn red. Perhaps Mary had read their thoughts.

"It's a good thing to think about your future. In fact, it's necessary to prepare yourself for the truest of loves."

"Mary understands us. The one who doesn't understand us is Jesus!" Naomi would burst out. So it seemed that the wisest thing to do was to prepare their hearts for the man who would choose them.

As time passed, one after the other, the young women of Nazareth became the brides of one or another young man. Jesus continued to be among the friends invited to the wedding.

In fact, living in Nazareth was just like living in any other town of Israel. Babies were born and they grew up. Young people learned a trade or housekeeping; they were married. And the old people passed away....

There were festivals to celebrate the harvest and national events. During some festivals people dressed in costume, and during others they asked God's forgiveness for their sins.

Mary shared wholeheartedly in these festivals. She shared in the joys and sufferings of her people.

She knew, however, that before all else she was Joseph's wife. He needed support, care and attention. Although their house was small and plain, she wanted it to always be clean and comfortable. She couldn't forget

this. Joseph had taken on the role of foster father, and he carried it out with intelligence, dedication and great love. But he was not like other fathers and husbands. Joseph had suffered for Jesus as much as Mary had. Jesus loved him and considered him a very dear friend. Now that Joseph was getting older, Jesus stayed even closer by his side.

The young men of Nazareth came over in the evenings to discuss daily events: politics, work, love. Jesus would invite Joseph to sit with them, and he'd ask him what he thought about different things. Jesus liked Joseph's simplicity and honesty. He thought of him as a just man, that is, an Israelite who thought and acted according to the teachings of the Bible.

One day Joseph fell ill, and Mary rushed to his side to take care of him. Jesus was also there to help him. For days the workshop stayed closed. It was more important to stay home and care for someone who was sick in the family. Every so often Mary would leave Jesus and Joseph alone. When she returned, she'd find Joseph happier and full of life.

One morning Jesus said to him, "Father, I have to thank you with all my heart for taking care of me as your son and for loving Mother. You will always be with us. Our family will be reunited in heaven."

Joseph took Jesus' hands and kissed them.

"Thank you, my son, my God. Take care of your mother. I'm going away happy. I'll be waiting for you."

And while Mary wiped Joseph's forehead, he peacefully fell asleep. Everyone in Nazareth mourned his death. Nothing was written on his tomb. But Matthew wrote in his Gospel: "He was a just man."

Today we greatly respect Joseph for his complete devotion to Jesus and Mary. He had loved and suffered for them in silence.

Soon Jesus went to open the workshop. He was taking Joseph's place. His strong hands did hard work, and were marked with calluses, scrapes and pain. His work apron was stained with tar and oil, and a piece of rope was usually hanging from his pocket. He gladly worked to support Mary, who was always busy at home. After work, he would find fresh water, newly washed clothes and a good meal.

So Jesus became the carpenter of Nazareth. His mother was touched every time she saw him bent over his work-table, measuring or hammering as Joseph used to do. He was the amazing son whom only she knew about. But how much longer would he stay close to her?

Mary and the First Miracle

It often happened that when Mary got up in the morning, she would find Jesus' mat folded up in a corner, but no Jesus. He would return when the sun began to light up the hillside. He would open the carpenter shop then because there was always someone who needed his help before going to work in the fields.

One morning when Mary saw Jesus arrive home, he looked like a ghost. As he walked, the sun's rays were shining from behind him. She waved to him but he didn't wave back.

"He's still talking with his Father," she thought. And she went back inside the house.

Jesus came in and sat down beside her. Mary took a deep breath. She sensed that she needed to be courageous. Then she said, "Son, I found your mat folded up. Didn't you sleep?"

"Yes, Mother, don't worry about that. My Father has given me the sign that it is time for me to go and find the lost sheep of the house of Israel. But you know how small our land is. We will see each other often."

Mary had trouble finding the right words to say to this son whom she loved so much. She wanted to tell him joyfully, "Go, my son, do what the Father asks of you. It is his will." But she couldn't, because she felt her heart breaking.

Jesus assured her, "I understand, Mother. But the time has come. John the Baptist is already announcing that the new kingdom is at hand. I will go to him."

"Go, son, go. We must do the will of your Father."

Jesus was about thirty years old when he went down to the Jordan River. There John was baptizing the people with water and inviting them to prepare the way for the Lord. He would say, "Convert, because the Kingdom is near."

Mary stayed in Nazareth. Her little house must have seemed too big for her now that she was alone.

People kept coming to visit her. They wanted to know when Jesus would be back. Mary didn't have the answer.

Months passed by. Then a man from Capernaum came to see Mary. He told her that he had heard from the caravan leaders that Jesus was on his way to Galilee.

Mary felt like springtime was knocking on the door of her house, on the door of her heart. She felt as if the sorrow of the long and hard winter had just been lifted from her shoulders. She hurried around the house to make sure that everything was ready for her son's return. Yes, yes everything was in place—only Jesus was missing.

One day she heard the children yelling loudly, "He's here! Jesus is here!"

She ran to the street and kissed him.

"You've never before been away from home for so long," Mary whispered.

"But now I'm here with you, Mother," Jesus smiled.

"You know, we've been invited to a wedding," Mary announced.

"Oh, where is it?" Jesus asked.

"In Cana."

"But I'm not alone, I have a few disciples," Jesus said. He turned and called to Peter, Andrew, Philip and Nathaniel. "I'll bring them along."

At the party Mary had Jesus by her side once again. Although he was concerned and friendly, he was also a bit quiet. Everyone drank to the happiness of the newlyweds with the good wine of Cana. They ate and drank heartily. The servants started to look worried.

Mary went to the kitchen. "What's going on? Is anything wrong?"

"Yes, yes...we didn't expect so many people. We've run out of wine."

"Oh!" exclaimed Mary. "That's right, Jesus' disciples also came with him. Wait a minute."

She went to Jesus and whispered, "Did you hear? They've run out of wine."

"What can I do about it, woman? My time has not yet come, you know."

Mary looked at him. Then she looked at the disciples who were just finishing the last drop of wine. She smiled. She went back into the kitchen and told the servants, "Do whatever he tells you to do!"

They ran to Jesus, who immediately told them, "Fill those jars up with water."

There were six big jars and each one could hold about twenty-two gallons of water. The servants filled them up, laughing at such a solution. Serving water to the guests wasn't quite the same thing as serving wine. But Mary had told them, "Do whatever he tells you to do," and so they did it. Then, following Jesus' instructions, the servants brought some of the water to the headwaiter. When he tasted it, he said to the groom, "Friend, usually the best wine is served first. Instead you've waited to serve the best wine until now that we've all had quite a bit. It's too bad. But this wine is so good that everyone will be happy to have some."

The servants also wanted to try the water-turned-wine. They thought it was very good, and felt that they should tell what Jesus had done.

And the party started up again.

His first miracle marked the beginning of the age of happiness that Jesus would bring to all of us. And that beginning was brought about through Mary. She knew her son well, and knew what he could do.
It was enough just to believe in him.

After seeing Jesus' power, the disciples believed in him and followed him.

Then Jesus went down into Capernaum, the city on the lake of Gennesaret. The disciples and Mary went with him.

The Beginning of a Mission

During this first year of Jesus' mission, he went back up to Jerusalem to celebrate Passover there. His mother Mary and the first disciples went with him.

They left Capernaum together and reached the holy city around holiday time. When he went up to the Temple, Jesus found people selling doves, sheep and oxen. He found people exchanging money.

Ever since his first visit to the Temple, Jesus had not liked that kind of market. Seeing the confusion and disorder, Jesus wanted to purify his Father's house. He made a whip out of some small pieces of rope. Striking to his right and left, he chased out the people who were selling sheep and oxen. He took the money from the money-changers and threw it to the ground. To the merchants he said, "Take your things away from here. Don't turn my Father's house into a marketplace!"

Everywhere sheep were bleating and oxen were bellowing. The merchants ran after their livestock to try and stop them. The people stood aside watching the rabbi who was powerful and bold enough to challenge the great marketplace of the Temple.

And then some merchants came up to Jesus. They were furious with him and yelled, "Hey, you! Who gave you the authority to do this? Give us a sign that you've been sent by God."

Jesus answered by challenging them, "If you destroy this Temple, I will rebuild it in three days."

Mary was not very far away. She was observing, listening, and remembering.... In the journal of her heart, many years earlier, she had written: "Tonight before lying down on his mat, Jesus said: 'Mother, the temple is here!' and he pointed to his body."

At that moment he was also pointing toward his body. Mary was sure that he was not talking about the Temple built by Herod forty-six years before. She recorded in the journal of her heart these new words that Jesus spoke. She didn't understand them, but one day their meaning would be clear to her.

Then Mary saw Jesus turn toward the poor, the blind and the crippled. She saw him comfort the poor and heal the sick. He was surrounded by great joy. He showed his ability to do things other people cannot do.

We know why Jesus was able to work these "signs" or miracles. He is the Son of God, just as the angel had told Mary. Jesus was carrying out his mission as Savior. He healed bodies in order to heal hearts. In fact, many people believed in Jesus and in the truth of his words.

There was a Jewish leader named Nicodemus. He asked Jesus if they could meet during the night for a discussion. Who knows why it had to be at night? Perhaps at that point Nicodemus wasn't brave enough to show his friendship with Jesus. Jesus understood him and promised to meet him. It was at that meeting with Nicodemus that Jesus made the most wonderful announcement. He said to him, "God loves the people of the world so much that he gave them his only Son, so that anyone who believes in him may share in never-ending joy. But first the Son has to be raised up."

Nicodemus was sincere in his search for the truth. Jesus helped him overcome his fears and become a faithful disciple.

Mary saw that many others did not believe in Jesus. They rejected him. From the beginning, Jesus' mission reflected the words Simeon had spoken to Mary: "He will be a sign of opposition." In other words, some people will believe in him, while others will be his enemies.

That was truly a Passover like no other, especially because Jesus was starting his mission of salvation there, in Jerusalem.

Mary believed that a new time of blessings was coming, although it wouldn't be an easy time. She saw that the disciples were very excited. Jesus was patient with them. He told them not to spread the word about his miracles. He didn't want people to follow him only because of his miracles. He told his disciples what he had told Nicodemus, "I must be raised up so that those who believe in me will have eternal life."

To be raised up meant to be placed on a cross in front of everyone. Is this what Jesus was talking about? Neither Mary nor the disciples could understand the meaning of his words. One day they would understand....

During the journey back home, Mary thought about all of this.

She knew that Jesus had to follow the path his Father had prepared for him. She, his mother, would go with him in spirit from her simple little house. She would be the Lord's servant so that her son's mission would reach people's hearts and convert them.

Who Is My Mother?

That summer Jesus traveled around Galilee and spoke in the synagogues. He left his audiences amazed. The people said that they had never seen such a teacher.

As he taught, Jesus healed the sick. There was no disease that could resist his hand and his will. He had such power that whenever he said, "This is my will," whatever he wanted would happen.

To the lepers who begged Jesus to heal them, Jesus said, "Such is my will: be healed," and the disease would disappear.

A centurion from Capernaum begged Jesus to heal his servant, who was paralyzed and suffering terribly. Jesus ordered, "Go, and if you believe, then so it will be." The servant was healed from far away.

Seeing all of these "signs," the crowds would run up to Jesus to listen to his words.

Even Mary rushed to hear the good news Jesus was announcing. He told the people that the time of mercy and love had arrived. God wanted everyone to know about it.

Mary, too, listened to Jesus' words and saw his deeds.

When the people recognized Mary, someone ran up to Jesus and said to him, "You know, your mother is here. She must want to see you."

Jesus was very happy that she was there. There was something he wanted everyone to know, "Do you know who my mother is, who my family is?"

He looked around waiting for an answer, but there was complete silence. Who could answer such a question?

"Here are my mother and my family: all of you who do the will of my Father in heaven."

The message is that those who do God's will, like Mary, will also be Jesus' mother, and sister, and brother. When we obey his words, Jesus grows inside of us, in our hearts.

How much we want Mary to help us receive in our hearts even one word spoken by Jesus, so we can live it every day!

Jesus kept preaching in Galilee and performing miracles. Every so often, Mary would hear some news about him.

Every time she heard something, she would record his teachings in her secret diary—the journal of her heart. Then she would look over Jesus' words and reflect on them. She could enjoy the message her son was bringing to the people.

One day, Jesus finally went back to Nazareth. Mary noticed how tired he looked, so she tried to help him regain some strength. She took a newly washed robe out of a chest. She prepared a bath for him so that he could refresh himself. It was Friday evening, before the holy day.

Jesus watched Mary's movements. When she came over with a fresh white robe for him to wear, he took her hands and kissed them. Two tears ran softly down his mother's cheeks.

When Jesus had put on the bright and clean-smelling robe, Mary sat down next to him. She hadn't done that in such a long time.

"I followed you all through Galilee," she said to him. "I saw the crowds that surrounded you. I saw your words planted in their hearts like a seed. You know, it seemed to me that in some hearts that seed didn't find earth to grow in. In others it was accepted, but sometimes there were worries that would steal away the seed like a hungry little bird.... But there were also watchful hearts that accepted the seed and let it take root and sprout. Oh, it seemed like the whole earth was becoming a marvelous field of golden wheat."

Jesus listened to her with joy. He was thinking that the heart that would receive the best fruit from the seed of his word was his mother's. Jesus said to her, "Mother, I will tell everyone this parable. People's hearts are truly like fields. Sometimes they are open, and sometimes they are reluctant to receive the seed.... But my seed is strong and it will find much fertile land. The world will be covered with its grain."

One Saturday at the Synagogue

The next day was Saturday. As usual, Jesus went to the synagogue, and Mary was with him. When the head rabbi invited him to the front, Jesus got up. He unrolled the scroll which was given to him. There was a passage from the prophet Isaiah. Jesus clearly read the words in Hebrew and translated them into Aramaic. These are the words Jesus read:

> The spirit of the Lord is upon me;
> for this reason he has anointed me with oil.
> He has sent me
> to bring good news to the poor,
> to proclaim freedom to the prisoners,
> to give sight to the blind,
> to restore freedom to the slaves,
> *and to preach a year of grace from the Lord.*

Then Jesus rolled up the parchment and sat down as the teachers do. All eyes in the synagogue were upon him, especially those of Mary. She had never heard him talk about the prophecies before.

Jesus began by saying, "Today this scripture which you have heard with your own ears has been fulfilled."

The people of Nazareth knew of the miracles Jesus had performed in Capernaum, in Naim, and in the surrounding areas. They had either heard people talk about them or else they had been there. And they had seen that Jesus had done what the prophet Isaiah spoke of. Words of grace, love and brotherhood came from his mouth. But where had he learned the things he was teaching?

"Listen!" they began to say, "he is Joseph's son, he's one of us. How come…?"

Jesus answered, "You will say to me: 'Do here in your own town what you have done in Capernaum.' You are asking each other where I came from, and you don't have faith. The proverb of our ancestors is true, 'No prophet is well-accepted in his own land.' What happened in the times of the prophet Elijah is happening now. There were many lepers in Israel, but none of them were healed. Instead, the Syrian man Naaman was healed. Although he was a pagan, he believed that the God of Israel could reveal himself through his prophet."

Mary saw the people of Nazareth suddenly jump to their feet in anger. How did Jesus dare accuse them of not believing? Threatening him, they forced him out of the town. They pushed him up to the edge of the hill which the town stood on. They wanted to throw him over the cliff.

Mary felt the sword of Simeon's prophecy piercing her heart. It made her weak, but she wanted to stay close by her son who was being insulted and perhaps would be killed.

Jesus had seen Mary while he was being pushed out of the synagogue, and he suffered because of her pain. His death would not come yet, but his mother already felt it. He thought of her when he found himself on the cliff. Jesus picked up the robe which the angry people had torn from him. He turned his back to the cliff. Then he quickly headed toward his house, passing through the crowd of people, who stood back in surprise.

Jesus found Mary waiting for him at home.

"My son!" she exclaimed. A radiant smile came to her face and her fear disappeared.

"Don't be afraid, Mother," Jesus said softly. "No one can take away my life. I will offer it myself when the Father wants me to."

And together Jesus and Mary blessed the holy day of Saturday using the words of the second psalm:

Why do people plot
and nations make plans against God
and against his Messiah?
He who is in heaven laughs
at them,
the Lord scorns them from
on high.
He speaks to them with anger:
"I have built my kingdom."
I will announce the Lord's
decree.
He told me: "You are my son,
I created you this day.
I will give you the people
of the world
and of all the earth."

It was written that the Father would glorify his Son. Mary felt a deep peace in her soul.

With Jesus as Passover Approaches

Mary had more long periods of waiting while Jesus traveled around the country. He even crossed the borders to bring salvation outside of Israel.

When he went down to Jerusalem for the Jewish holidays, he would be away from home for months.

Every so often one of his disciples would knock on Mary's door.

She always welcomed them. She was eager to learn how the seed of salvation was being received. She wanted to know how the word which Jesus was spreading in Judea and in Jerusalem was being accepted.

She knew that, unfortunately, many hearts were as hard as rocks. They would not let Jesus' word penetrate them. Some of the people waged war on him. They denied his miracles and opposed his teachings. They accused him of wanting to destroy the Temple. Most of all, they accused him of wanting to be God. They didn't know that he *was* God.

Mary also knew that Jesus had gone down to Bethany, the village of Mary and Martha, to "reawaken" his friend Lazarus who had died. Jesus brought Lazarus back to life! His enemies saw that the people were following him as a prophet, and they decided to kill him. In fact, only a great prophet could bring life to a man who had been dead for four days.

Since it was almost time for the Passover, Mary made the journey to Jerusalem with many other pilgrims. Her relatives were happy to have her with them. Mary sensed that they were worried because they feared for Jesus' life.

At that time Jesus was in Bethany, in Lazarus' house. He came every day to the holy city to teach the people.

One of these mornings Mary went out to the street which led up to the Temple. There she waited for him. A crowd had gathered to honor Jesus. They greeted him shouting, "Hosanna! Hosanna to the son of David!"

A group of children near Mary were yelling the loudest. They were holding olive and palm branches. They were shouting around Jesus, who was riding a donkey up to the Temple.

Mary forgot about her pain for a moment. She let herself be carried away with the excitement of the crowd. She also held an olive branch and waved it, shouting out, "Hosanna to the son of David!"

In her secret heart journal, Mary had recorded the words of the angel, who promised that her baby would sit on the throne of David, his father. Jesus was truly one of David's descendants. He deserved the throne and more. But the leaders of the people didn't like what they saw in Jesus' triumph.

"Look," they said, "they're all following him." And they were trying to figure out how to calm the excited children.

"Let them keep chanting," Jesus said. "If the children stop shouting, the stones will cry out."

Then Jesus moved to where he could not be seen, because the leaders wanted to kill him.

At the Last Supper

Jesus knew that the time had come for him to leave this world and join his Father. It was his Passover. He wanted to celebrate it in the city with his relatives because his mother was with them. His relatives had welcomed him many times before into their home for the holidays. He chose two of the apostles (the apostles were Jesus' closest followers) and sent them to get everything ready: the lamb, the bitter herbs, the eggs, the unleavened bread and the wine.

When evening came around, Jesus met his apostles. His mother was there to welcome him, while one of his relatives offered him some water to wash his hands and feet.

It had been Mary's job to decorate the largest room in the house with the holiday candles. She had gone about her work with joy and sadness. Mary hoped for something good to happen during that Passover. But she knew that there would be a high price to pay.

When everyone had taken their places, Jesus wrapped a towel around his waist. He poured some water in a basin and began to wash the apostles' feet. Then he dried them with the towel he had wrapped around himself.

Mary saw Jesus pass humbly and eagerly from one of his friends to the next. He, their Teacher, bowed down in front of them. He wanted them to understand that they should do good to their brothers and sisters. If someone wanted to be the most important in God's kingdom, he would have

to be last. He would have to be the servant of all the others.

Mary watched all of Jesus' actions. She didn't miss the look of sorrow on his face when she heard him say, "One of you will betray me." She didn't ask, "Who will it be?" These were Jesus' friends. Mary didn't want to think that one of them would betray him. Maybe this was the pain which was weighing down his heart.

Then Jesus thanked God for all the gifts he had given to his people. He thanked God for saving the people of Israel at the Sea of Reeds, and for giving the holy Law. Jesus raised the cup of blessing to his lips, then passed it around to his friends.

Mary realized that after the Hebrew dinner, her son continued with a new celebration. She saw him take the unleavened bread, give thanks, break it, and give it to his apostles. He said, "This is my body which will be given up for you. Do this in memory of me."

She also saw Jesus take the cup of wine. While he poured it for them, she heard him say, "This chalice is the new covenant of my blood which will be shed for you."

That night, the apostles were the first to receive Jesus' own body and blood in Holy Communion.

Mary understood that Jesus' words and actions were a sign of the total gift of himself to the Father. On the next day Jesus would offer his life for the salvation of all people.

The dinner was finished and the songs of praise had ended. Jesus and his apostles left the supper room and went to a garden called Gethsemane.

Mary stayed home and thought about everything that had happened. She believed that Jesus was sharing a new grace with her. This grace would help her bear all of the pain which she would suffer very soon. In fact, the pain would begin that very night.

We can imagine that on that night Mary saw all the people who would receive Holy Communion in the future. She saw Jesus giving himself to children and young people. He would help them be his witnesses.

Today we, too, want to be united with Jesus in the Eucharist. We thank him for all his gifts, especially for being with us always.

I am sure that in that hour of joy Jesus' mother also saw you. She wants you to be able to feel the same joy they felt that night, every time you receive Communion.

With Her Dying Son

When dawn came, Mary heard someone knocking on her door. She ran to see who it was: it was John, the youngest of Jesus' apostles. Out of breath and upset, he burst out, "They've arrested Jesus!"

"What? Arrested him?" Mary cried out.

"Yes. The guards came, led by Judas. They tied Jesus up and took him to the religious leaders. In front of the high priest Caiaphas, Jesus said he was the Christ, the Son of God. I was there with Peter. Now they have taken Jesus to Pilate, the Roman governor."

Mary had already grabbed her cape and was heading out the door.

"Wait!" one of her relatives called after her. "I'll come with you and John."

Together they went to the governor's building.

Mary saw Jesus there. He was in front of Pilate with his hands tied and his head down. His clothes were all roughed up, and his face was covered with drops of blood.

"They've hit him! My Lord, have mercy," Mary said softly. She was finding it hard to breathe and felt a knot tighten in her stomach. But she wanted to stay, to share in her son's suffering. She wanted to give Jesus the comfort of having her close by, if he should notice that she was there.

Pilate, the governor, questioned Jesus and was sure that he was innocent. But because of the accusations made by some of the people, he wanted Jesus to prove his innocence. Instead Jesus remained silent and thoughtful.

Then Pilate looked out from the balcony of the courtroom. He said to the crowd that had gathered, "Tomorrow is your holiday. On such occasions it is customary for me to free a prisoner. Do you want me to free your king?"

The crowd yelled, "No, not him! Free Barabbas for us!" Barabbas was a bandit.

So Pilate ordered the soldiers to whip Jesus. The soldiers took him to the courtyard.

Mary saw him come back after a short time, and her heart skipped a beat. It wasn't enough to make him suffer with the whipping. They had also made fun of him by placing a purple rag over his shoulders like a royal mantle and by pressing a crown of thorns on his head.

Mary must have suffered so much! Her pain was very deep because her love for Jesus was very deep. In fact, no one has ever or will ever love Jesus as much as his mother did.

While she was feeling her son's pain, Mary heard the crowd yell to Pilate, "Crucify him! Crucify him! If you don't, then you're no friend of Caesar."

"We have a law, and according to this law he must die, because he's called himself the Son of God!"

Pilate was frightened because Jesus had claimed to be the Son of God. What if it were true? He hesitated a moment. Then, so that people would not complain about him to Caesar, Pilate gave in to the crowd. He told the people that Jesus would be crucified.

Mary was still in front of the courthouse when Jesus came out. He was carrying the wooden cross on his shoulders. She went as close to him as she could. Jesus looked at her. The look of pain he saw on Mary's face said more to him than any words could say. Mary saw in her Jesus' eyes his silent acceptance of his sufferings.

Together they walked to Calvary. The mother's presence gave strength to the son. The son's presence helped the mother accept his suffering, although it was very painful for her.

John, Mary of Clopas, and Mary Magdalen were with Mary. They could not find words to comfort her. What could they say at a time like that?

Soon they reached Calvary. There the Roman soldiers stripped Jesus of his clothing and laid him on the cross. Showing no mercy at all for him or for his mother, they nailed his hands and feet to the cross.

There will never be a mother who will suffer as much as Jesus' mother did. Her son whom the people were killing was not just a man—he was God, our God.

Let us stay close to Mary, the mother of sorrows, who felt her son's pain. Let us thank Mary for saying "yes" to God's will over and over again, even when this was very hard to do.

One Mother for Everyone

It was around noon. A frightening darkness covered the city of Jerusalem when the soldiers raised the cross. A sigh of pity swept through the crowd at the sight of Jesus. He had terrible wounds in his hands and feet. The high priests, however, were angry because there was a sign on the cross which said, "Jesus of Nazareth, King of the Jews."

They were saying: "But he's not the king of the Jews. That's what he'd like to be! Pilate is making us look like fools!"

Furious, they went to complain to Pilate. But Pilate said, "I've written what I've written!" And he refused to take down the sign.

Even Mary saw what had been written. From the journal in her heart she remembered the angel's words, "You will have a son and you will name him Jesus.... God will give him the throne of David and his kingdom will have no end." That kingdom, though, would not be an earthly one. But it would be a kingdom of love. It would be a kingdom for the gentle-hearted, for the peacemakers, for those who love their neighbors. It would be for those who would see the cross and say with Jesus: "Father, forgive them."

"My son," Mary prayed, "open up heaven to everyone. Receive me among those who love you."

Mary moved close to the cross and stood there, straight and strong. Her eyes were fixed on Jesus' suffering face. All around her she heard words that made fun of Jesus.

"If you are the Son of God, then come down from the cross!"

"You saved others, now save yourself!"

"You said that you can destroy the Temple and rebuild it in three days! Go ahead, come down from the cross if you can!"

Mary remembered that Jesus had once said, "If you destroy this Temple...," not "I will destroy this Temple." The people who crucified Jesus were destroying the true Temple of God, Jesus' body. In her heart, Mary was

certain that the other part of what Jesus said would come true: "I will rebuild it in three days."

She couldn't understand, though, how the crowd could be so cruel toward Jesus. He had healed the lame, given sight to the blind, given bread and fish to the poor who had followed him to hear his words, had brought life back to a boy, a little girl and his friend Lazarus. So many people had seen his miracles.... So why, then, did they hate him?...

Mary kept looking at her son. Even though he was suffering so much, Jesus was still patient and forgiving. He was praying softly, "Father, forgive them, because they don't know what they are doing."

Mary was thinking about these words when she saw Jesus looking around. Maybe he was looking for his friends, the apostles. They were not there because their fear was greater than their love for him. And Jesus felt that pain deep in his heart. But he saw his mother, John, Mary Magdalen, his mother's relative—Mary of Clopas, and also Nicodemus and Joseph of Arimathea.

Mary noticed that Jesus was looking mostly at herself and John. She got as close as she could to him and heard him say with great effort, "Woman, here is your son."

Then looking at John, Jesus said, "Here is your mother."

Jesus had fulfilled his last duty as a son by helping Mary. At the same time he gave her as a tender mother to every man and woman, because John represented all of us.

So, you and I and all of our brothers and sisters can turn to Mary at any time. We can turn to Mary in times of joy or suffering, when things go right or when they don't, when we feel at peace with God and when—who knows why—we feel as if God is no longer on our side....

Mary, our mother in heaven, will welcome us tenderly. She will help us be brave. She will help us to live for Jesus and for others.

In his suffering Jesus had shown his love for his Father. Now he prayed, "Everything is done. Father, I entrust my soul into your hands."

And bowing his head, he breathed for the last time. It was three o'clock in the afternoon.

Mary hugged the cross and kissed Jesus' feet, which were covered with blood. She believed that she had been the first one to be saved by his divine blood.

Since it was the eve of Passover, and the holiday was about to begin, Joseph of Arimathea got permission from Pilate to take Jesus' body down from the cross.

Mary was there to receive her son on her lap one last time. She carefully removed the thorns from his head. She wiped the blood from his face, and cleaned away the blood and water coming out of the open wound in his side.

While her tears were falling on her son's lifeless body, she said: "Jesus died because of his love for people. But he promised us that he would soon be with us again."

Joseph of Arimathea had prepared a tomb which had just been carved out of rock. It was close by. He wrapped the body of Jesus in a new sheet and placed it in the tomb.

Mary entered the tomb. Her hands trembled as she hugged Jesus' body. Then Joseph and the others led her out, closed the tomb with a boulder, and went back to the city.

Mary knew that Jesus, the very precious "pearl" who had grown within her, came from God. Nothing, not even death, could destroy him. But now they all had to wait for Jesus to come out of the dark tomb and shine in God's light.

The Joy of Seeing Jesus Again

When she went back to Jerusalem, Mary noticed the houses already shining with the holiday lights.

"This night will pass," she said to herself. "Then Jesus will return."

She felt that her son's great pain and her own had already disappeared.

Peter, Andrew, Bartholomew, Jude and the others came to her mind. She also thought of Judas....

"He will not come back, that poor man who dreamed of a world built on violence.... But he too at times really loved Jesus and he served the group.... The others...will return...."

In fact, late at night, someone came knocking at the door of the house where Mary was staying. The Passover dinner was almost over.

"Shalom, brother. Come in!" said the father of the family. "Welcome, on this night when God saved us from our oppressors."

The head of the family didn't know that God was truly saving his people that very night. The lamb's blood was only a symbol. The true blood of salvation was from the lamb, Jesus.

The man at the door took off his cloak. His face looked worn out from crying. His hair was all out of place as if he had walked through a storm. It was Peter.

"Peace!" he said. "Where is Mary?"

"She is praying."

"Could I see her?"

"Wouldn't you like to sit with us for a while first?"

"I must see her."

They let him go into the room where Mary was praying. He ran to throw himself at Mary's feet.

"I betrayed Jesus, Mother. I swore to him that I would follow him even until death. Instead I claimed that I didn't know him. But I loved him."

"And you still love him, Peter. Love is stronger than our weaknesses. It's easy to think that we are stronger than we actually are. Jesus has made you think about this.... But now you've cried enough. Be strong!"

In his heart Peter heard the words Jesus had spoken on the night of the Last Supper. He said them out loud, "You will deny my three times, but when you have repented, help your brothers."

"My son," Mary said, "you will have another chance to love, serve and witness to Jesus. You will know him better once he has given you his Holy Spirit. We will wait for the third day. Then he will be with us again. Do you remember? He told us, 'On the third day, I will rise again.'"

"Yes, Mother, he will rise. I believe it."

On that Passover Saturday the other apostles also came to cry to Jesus' mother. They were sorry they had abandoned Jesus in his time of suffering. And they remembered the acts of love Jesus had offered to each one of them.

"You see," Mary said, "Jesus is not dead. He lives on in the loving actions he left us. We will see him again. Oh, how our hearts will rejoice when that time comes!"

Mary was no longer crying because now her son was resting in peace. And her faith strengthened the faith of the disciples.

"Yes," she said, "tomorrow will mark the beginning of a new world."

Mary wanted to see Jesus so badly that she would have pushed the sun to make it move more quickly through the sky.

Evening came, and then the deep night. Finally the darkness gave way to the gentle rays of dawn.

The other women who had been there when Jesus died took scented oils and went to the tomb to honor his body. They hadn't done this sooner because it was forbidden on the holiday.

In the garden the boulder which had blocked the entrance to the tomb had been pushed aside. The body of Jesus had been taken away.

A young boy dressed in white was standing there. He said, "I know you're looking for Jesus. He is not here. He has risen! Don't look for the living among the dead!"

It was the first Easter.

The women got scared and ran away. Mary Magdalen, however, did not want to leave. She stayed by the tomb and cried. It was then that she heard the voice she knew so well.

"Mary!"

She turned around and saw Jesus.

"Oh, my Master!" she exclaimed.

"Don't touch me! Go to my brothers and tell them that I am waiting in Galilee."

And while Mary Magdalen was trying to understand what was going on, Jesus left.

Jesus had given Mary Magdalen the duty of telling his disciples he had risen. But who would bring the message to his mother?

The Gospel writers didn't think it was necessary to tell us this.

We like to think that Jesus himself went to his mother. We can imagine that the meeting between the mother and her son happened like this.

At the break of dawn Mary had put on her white gown, and waited for Jesus. Then she saw him coming toward her, clothed in God's light. When he greeted her, she was aware of a new sweetness in his voice.

"Peace be with you, Mother! I have risen and I am with you again. Death has been defeated by life."

Mary's eyes opened wide to gaze at Jesus. Her faith and joy were bubbling over because his face no longer had the signs of death. The wounds in his hands, feet and side had disappeared. In their place there was beautiful light.

Mary was overwhelmed with joy. Jesus reached out his hands to her and she covered them with her own. She said softly, "Son!" as she kissed his blessed hands.

"You have drunk from the cup of my suffering, Mother. Share also in the joy of my victory. The body which you have given me has shed the blood which will save the world."

"My Son!" Mary whispered.

But Jesus was already raising his hand to bless her. Then he disappeared.

When Mary Magdalen arrived, all out of breath from running, she found Mary seated in the garden, bathed in sunlight. Mary Magdalen stopped and exclaimed, "Jesus has come back! Yes, the tomb is empty, and I saw him. He called me by name."

Then Mary stood up and prayed:

Alleluia!

My soul praises the Lord.

My spirit rejoices in God
because he has glorified his Son.
God brought him back from the dead.
And he has made him the resurrection
and the life of every person.
Those who believe in him will live happily forever.

John and Peter rushed off to the tomb to see for themselves what Mary Magdalen had told them. They came back to tell Mary: "He's risen! He's risen!"

It's not easy to believe that someone could rise from the dead! The apostles were closed in the room where they had last shared the Last Supper with Jesus. They talked about it all day. Then the two disciples who had walked to the village of Emmaus several hours earlier returned.

"We have seen Jesus" they said. "He walked with us and sat at our table. At first we didn't know it was him. But when he broke the bread with his act of blessing, we recognized him. By then he had already disappeared."

At that moment Jesus appeared among the group of his followers and greeted them.

"Peace be with you!"

They were frightened. How could it be true?

"Why do you still have doubts in your hearts?" Jesus gently asked. "Look at my hands and feet. It's really me!"

The apostles didn't know what to think or do.

"Please," Jesus said, "give me something to eat."

Looking at him in amazement, they gave him some roasted fish. He ate it in front of them and said, "You know that it is written that: 'The Christ will have to suffer and come back from the dead on the third day. In his name, the forgiveness of sins will be announced to all people.' Remember to stay in the city until I send you the promised Spirit from the Father."

Jesus appeared to them for forty days. Mary enjoyed his presence even though she knew that she would lose him again. He would have to go back to the Father.

Together with his mother, Jesus gathered his friends near Bethany on the Mount of Olives. After he had talked with them a while, he said, "All power in heaven and earth has been given to me. Go all around the world. Make all people my disciples by baptizing them in the name of the Father and of the Son and of the Holy Spirit, so that they may be saved."

Jesus lifted up his hands and blessed them. Then he moved upward, away from them and ascended into heaven.

Jesus knew how important his mother's faith would be in guiding his friends. He left her to stay here on earth for a while.

Mother of the Newborn Church

That day the apostles came down from the mountain full of joy. Jesus had left them, but he had promised to send the Holy Spirit. They felt that they greatly needed the Spirit. Without the Holy Spirit's strength and light, how would they be able to carry out the mission Jesus had given them?

"Mother," Peter said to Mary, "we'll stay with you. Please guide us while we wait for the Holy Spirit whom Jesus promised."

In Jerusalem they gathered once again in the large supper room. There Jesus had shown his love by changing the bread and wine into his body and blood.

Everyone came together: the apostles, the women and the other disciples. They prayed for the Holy Spirit to come. Together they remembered Jesus' words and asked the Spirit to let Jesus' words be a light on their path.

The apostles and disciples knew only about the events that had happened during the last three years of Jesus' life. While they remembered his words, they also wanted to learn about the life Jesus led before he met them. Who could tell them more about those earlier years than his mother? They begged Mary to speak to them about Jesus.

Mary knew that she was being asked to bear witness to her son. She opened up her secret "journal" and relived Jesus' life. She started from the moment when God had wrapped her in his power and made her Jesus' mother.

Mary had often turned to the journal of her heart to help her to understand what other things Jesus would want to say to his disciples. Those were wonderful hours for her. With the light of the Holy Spirit she kept discovering more and more about her son. He was so different from any other son in the world!

Even for Mary there were mysterious missing pieces in her knowledge of Jesus' life. In fact, Jesus isn't only a man—he is God. No human being, not even his mother, would ever understand him completely. Mary would simply say that although she was his mother, she felt like one of his disciples.

The disciples realized that God had a very special love for Mary and had given her many gifts. Some of these were so special that God would never give them to any other person.

On the fiftieth day after Easter, Mary and the disciples were all gathered together. They suddenly heard a loud roaring, like a wind blowing with great force. Then fire in the shape of tongues appeared above each one of them.

Suddenly the disciples realized that the wind and fire were signs of the presence of the Holy Spirit who was entering into their hearts.

They were filled with joy and were no longer afraid. Every one of them felt a deep peace inside. They felt the need to tell everyone about the risen Jesus.

Peter was watching Mary. Jesus' promise to send the Holy Spirit had also been fulfilled in her.

In fact, the Holy Spirit, the Giver of Life, who had visited her many years before to make her the mother of Jesus, was returning to fill her with more grace. He was filling her heart with love for the Church, which was being born that day. The Church would be Jesus' mystical body. You and I, all of our friends,

and all Christians, are members of the Church. We became members at our baptism.

Mary looked at Jesus' disciples, and her glance was like a gift of new love. She said, "My children, today we rejoice in the name of the Lord. He is visiting us with his Spirit of truth. According to the promise, the Holy Spirit will show us the meaning of Jesus' words. And in the joy of the Spirit, we obey these words. Let's go! Our sisters and brothers are calling us. Let's tell everyone about God's saving love in Jesus."

Guided by the Holy Spirit, the apostles and disciples ran outside to meet the crowd that had heard the crashing of the wind and had come to see what was happening.

Peter, the fisherman from Galilee, rose to his feet. The Holy Spirit made him understand the meaning of Jesus' life in a whole new way. Peter said to the people, "Brothers and sisters! May you know that Jesus of Nazareth, whom you nailed to the cross and killed, has been brought to life by God. All of us here are witnesses to this. The man Jesus whom you crucified, is the Lord of the world."

Mary stayed in the supper room and was listening to Peter's voice. "It is the work of the Holy Spirit," she said. "Peter is a new man."

He really was! The fear he had felt the night Jesus was arrested had turned into courage. Peter was happy to tell others about Jesus, the Son of God.

Speaking in the language of his people, Peter didn't know that the Holy Spirit was working a miracle in him. All of the foreigners who had come from far away to celebrate the feast understood him perfectly. In fact, they heard him speak in their own language. They were sorry for their sins, and believed in Jesus who had died and risen. So they asked to be baptized.

Mary believed that the disciples were like good seed. The seed was growing in the sun and spreading. She would help take care of that seed.

You are also one of the seeds Mary loves. Stay close to her, because where Mary is, there is the Holy Spirit. The Spirit brings joy, peace and brotherhood. The Holy Spirit helps us love and praise Jesus and spread his words of love.

Mary in Heaven

Guided by the Holy Spirit, the apostles and disciples announced that Jesus had died and risen. First they preached in Jerusalem and then in the cities and villages of Judea, Samaria and Galilee. Next the Spirit brought them far away, beyond the borders of their land. They met Greeks, Romans, Egyptians and people from India and Spain.

All over the earth the apostles and disciples taught people about Jesus. Jesus was becoming known and loved by all kinds of people: the rich and the poor, the powerful and the slaves. Everyone was becoming united by God's new law, the commandment of love.

Mary, the mother of all people, stayed in Jerusalem to help the followers of Jesus who were leaving and to welcome those who were returning from difficult missions. The Holy Spirit gave the apostles courage to bear sufferings and opposition. The apostles brought everyone the bread of life and the truth that saves.

When John became the leader of the Church of Ephesus, he brought Mary there with him. She was the first person to bear witness to Jesus. Everyone wanted to listen to her words. When Mary spoke to the people, they felt Jesus' presence and love in her.

But, Mary's time on earth seemed to be reaching its end. She was accompanied back to Jerusalem.

We can imagine that Mary was still always concerned about others, even while she was waiting to be reunited with Jesus. She would go to visit the sick, to comfort the suffering, to help the poor, and to support the weak.

Most of all, everyone wanted help from her to understand Jesus better. And Mary would offer this gift with such great joy! These final gifts were the last jewels placed in her glorious crown.

One day she asked the women who were disciples of Jesus to come to her. Mary kissed them one by one and spoke words of love to each one.

Then the apostles who were in Jerusalem came. They prayed together.

"Come, Oh Lord!"

"Come, Lord Jesus!"

Mary was ready. As on the day the angel came, she whispered to God, "Here I am! Yes!"

"Mother! Mother! Mary! Stay with us a while longer!" begged the women.

But she was already with her Son.

The women prepared Mary's body. The community of Jerusalem and those close by came to cry in silence near the Mother.

Mary's body, which had carried Jesus, was not left to decay. God the Father took her, body and soul, into the glory of heaven.

When we think of Mary, we must think of her as being close to Jesus. Mary talks to Jesus about us. She prays for our needs, and asks him to bless us as he used to bless the children of the Holy Land.

And Jesus listens to his mother's wishes. He blesses his children and fills them with his Holy Spirit. We belong to Jesus. He fills us with joy because joy is the gift of the Spirit who lives in us.

In order to give us this joy, Jesus became the pearl of Mary. Jesus became Mary's son and our brother. We can never be grateful enough to Jesus for coming to us. We can never be grateful enough to Mary for being Jesus' mother.

Pauline BOOKS & MEDIA

ALASKA
750 West 5th Ave., Anchorage, AK 99501   907-272-8183
CALIFORNIA
3908 Sepulveda Blvd., Culver City, CA 90230   310-397-8676
5945 Balboa Ave., San Diego, CA 92111   619-565-9181
46 Geary Street, San Francisco, CA 94108   415-781-5180
FLORIDA
145 S.W. 107th Ave., Miami, FL 33174   305-559-6715
HAWAII
1143 Bishop Street, Honolulu, HI 96813   808-521-2731
ILLINOIS
172 North Michigan Ave., Chicago, IL 60601   312-346-4228
LOUISIANA
4403 Veterans Memorial Blvd., Metairie, LA 70006   504-887-7631
MASSACHUSETTS
50 St. Paul's Ave., Jamaica Plain, Boston, MA 02130
 617-522-8911
Rte. 1, 885 Providence Hwy., Dedham, MA 02026   617-326-5385
MISSOURI
9804 Watson Rd., St. Louis, MO 63126   314-965-3512
NEW JERSEY
561 U.S. Route 1, Wick Plaza, Edison, NJ 08817   908-572-1200
NEW YORK
150 East 52nd Street, New York, NY 10022   212-754-1110
78 Fort Place, Staten Island, NY 10301   718-447-5071
OHIO
2105 Ontario Street (at Prospect Ave.), Cleveland, OH 44115
 610-621-9427
PENNSYLVANIA
Northeast Shopping Center, 9171-A Roosevelt Blvd.
Philadelphia, PA 19114; 215-676-9494
SOUTH CAROLINA
243 King Street, Charleston, SC 29401   803-577-0175
TENNESSEE
4811 Poplar Ave., Memphis, TN 38117   901-761-2987
TEXAS
114 Main Plaza, San Antonio, TX 78205   210-224-8101
VIRGINIA
1025 King Street, Alexandria, VA 22314   703-549-3806
CANADA
3022 Dufferin Street, Toronto, Ontario, Canada M6B 3T5
 416-781-9131